JOHN LENNON

★ ★ ★ ★ ★ ★ ★ ★ ★ ★ ★ ★ ★ ★ ★ ★

JOHN LENNON

★ ★

BRUCE W. CONORD

CHELSEA HOUSE PUBLISHERS

New York ★ Philadelphia

CHELSEA HOUSE PUBLISHERS

EDITORIAL DIRECTOR   Richard Rennert
EXECUTIVE MANAGING EDITOR   Karyn Gullen Browne
EXECUTIVE EDITOR   Sean Dolan
COPY CHIEF   Robin James
PICTURE EDITOR   Adrian G. Allen
ART DIRECTOR   Robert Mitchell
MANUFACTURING DIRECTOR   Gerald Levine
PRODUCTION COORDINATOR   Marie Claire Cebrián-Ume

Pop Culture Legends
SENIOR EDITOR   Kathy Kuhtz

Staff for **JOHN LENNON**
COPY EDITOR   Danielle Janusz
EDITORIAL ASSISTANT   Mary B. Sisson
PICTURE RESEARCHER   Pat Burns
DESIGNER   Basia Niemczyc
COVER ILLUSTRATION   Bradford Brown

First Printing

1 3 5 7 9 8 6 4 2

Library of Congress Cataloging-in-Publication Data

Conord, Bruce W.
John Lennon/Bruce W. Conord.
p. cm.—(Pop culture legends)
Includes bibliographical references and index.
Summary: A biography of the famous singer, songwriter, and member of the Beatles.
ISBN 0-7910-1739-7
        0-7910-1740-0 (pbk.)
1. Lennon, John, 1940–1980—Juvenile literature. 2. Rock musicians—Biography—Juvenile literature. [1. Lennon, John, 1940–1980. 2. Musicians. 3. Rock music.] I. Title. II. Series.
ML3930.L34C68 1993   92-39113
782.42166'092—dc20   CIP
[B]   AC MN

FRONTISPIECE:
John Lennon performs at a concert in Hamburg, West Germany, circa 1964.

Contents ★

A Reflection of Ourselves

Leeza Gibbons

I ENJOY A RARE PERSPECTIVE on the entertainment industry. From my window on popular culture, I can see all that sizzles and excites. I have interviewed legends who have left us, such as Bette Davis and Sammy Davis, Jr., and have brushed shoulders with the names who have caused a commotion with their sheer outrageousness, like Boy George and Madonna. Whether it's by nature or by design, pop icons generate interest, and I think they are a mirror of who we are at any given time.

Who are *your* heroes and heroines, the people you most admire? Outside of your own family and friends, to whom do you look for inspiration and guidance, as examples of the type of person you would like to be as an adult? How do we decide who will be the most popular and influential members of our society?

You may be surprised by your answers. According to recent polls, you will probably respond much differently than your parents or grandparents did to the same questions at the same age. Increasingly, world leaders such as Winston Churchill, John F. Kennedy, Franklin D. Roosevelt, and evangelist Billy Graham have been replaced by entertainers, athletes, and popular artists as the individuals whom young people most respect and admire. In surveys taken during each of the past 15 years, for example, General Norman Schwarzkopf was the only world leader chosen as the number-one hero among high school students. Other names on the elite list joined by General Schwarzkopf included Paula Abdul, Michael Jackson, Michael Jordan, Eddie Murphy, Burt Reynolds, and Sylvester Stallone.

More than 30 years have passed since Canadian sociologist Marshall McLuhan first taught us the huge impact that the electronic media has had on how we think, learn, and understand—as well as how we choose our heroes. In the 1960s, Pop artist Andy Warhol predicted that there would soon come a time when every American would be famous for 15 minutes. But if it is easier today to achieve Warhol's 15 minutes of fame, it is also much harder to hold on to it. Reputations are often ruined as quickly as they are made.

And yet, there remain those artists and performers who continue to inspire and instruct us in spite of changes in world events, media technology, or popular tastes. Even in a society as fickle and fast moving as our own, there are still those performers whose work and reputation endure, pop culture legends who inspire an almost religious devotion from their fans.

Why do the works and personalities of some artists continue to fascinate us while others are so quickly forgotten? What, if any, qualities do they share that enable them to have such power over our lives? There are no easy answers to these questions. The artists and entertainers profiled in this series often have little more in common than the enormous influence that each of them has had on our lives.

Some offer us an escape. Artists such as actress Marilyn Monroe comedian Groucho Marx, and writer Stephen King have used glamour, humor, or fantasy to help us escape from our everyday lives. Others present us with images that are all too recognizable. The uncompromising realism of actor and director Charlie Chaplin and folk singer Bob Dylan challenges us to confront and change the things in our world that most disturb us.

Some offer us friendly, reassuring experiences. The work of animator Walt Disney and late-night talk show host Johnny Carson, for example, provides us with a sense of security and continuity in a changing world. Others shake us up. The best work of composer John Lennon and actor James Dean will always inspire their fans to question and reevaluate the world in which they live.

It is also hard to predict the kind of life that a pop culture legend will lead, or how he or she will react to fame. Popular singers Michael Jackson

and Prince carefully guard their personal lives from public view. Other performers, such as popular singer Madonna, enjoy putting their private lives before the public eye.

What these artists and entertainers do share, however, is the rare ability to capture and hold the public's imagination in a world dominated by mass media and disposable celebrity. In spite of their differences, each of them has somehow managed to achieve legendary status in a popular culture that values novelty and change.

The books in this series examine the lives and careers of these and other pop culture legends, and the society that places such great value on their work. Each book considers the extraordinary talent, the stubborn commitment, and the great personal sacrifice required to create work of enduring quality and influence in today's world.

As you read these books, ask yourself the following questions: How are the careers of these individuals shaped by their society? What role do they play in shaping the world? And what is it that so captivates us about their lives, their work, or the images they present?

Hopefully, by studying the lives and achievements of these pop culture legends, we will learn more about ourselves.

"Beatlemania"

A SENSE OF EXCITEMENT and anticipation swept across the United States as teenagers listened to their local rock and roll radio stations. Thousands of young fans gathered at Kennedy Airport in New York on a cold and gray winter morning, Friday, February 7, 1964, to wait for the arrival of the Beatles. The British band, whose members were John Lennon, Paul McCartney, George Harrison, and Ringo Starr (the stage name of Richard Starkey), had skyrocketed to the top of America's musical charts with the release of their new record, "I Want To Hold Your Hand." This was the Beatles' first appearance on American soil.

"Beatlemania," the name given to the overwhelmingly enthusiastic reaction of the fans who heard the Beatles play, had already swept England. Young men imitated the Beatles' long hairstyle and collarless suit jackets. Young women screamed and called out the names of John, Paul, George, and Ringo—their cries were so loud that during concerts it was impossible at times to hear the music. Adoring fans mobbed the Beatles whenever they appeared in public.

On February 7, 1964, John Lennon (wearing hat) and the other members of the band wave to fans who have come to greet them at New York's Kennedy International Airport at the start of the Beatles' first tour in the United States.

In November 1963, the Beatles, wearing the hairstyle and collarless suits that they made popular, take a break during a concert. From left to right are: John Lennon (the group's unofficial leader), George Harrison, Paul McCartney, and Ringo Starr.

Capitol, the record company that distributed the Beatles' records in the United States, spent $50,000 in advertising to build up excitement among America's teens. Capitol flooded the country with posters, bumper stickers, and buttons printed with the words: The Beatles Are Coming!

Radio stations also promoted the Beatles' arrival. Some disc jockeys had been given a list of questions and a prerecorded tape of the Beatles' answers to those questions, which allowed each radio personality to promote themselves as personal friends of the group. One of the largest rock and roll radio stations in the country at the time, WMCA in New York, kept its listeners dangling in anticipation while the disc jockeys tracked the progress

of the Beatles' Pan Am flight across the Atlantic. "It is now 8:17, Beatle time," the announcer said breathlessly. "They are now eleven hundred miles offshore. . . . The temperature is 32 Beatle degrees."

Meanwhile, on the plane, the four Beatles laughed and joked with the flight attendants. John Lennon, the group's unofficial leader, sat next to his wife, Cynthia, and chain-smoked cigarettes. Tall and handsome with dark brown eyes, the 24-year-old wore his long brown hair in the mop-top style that he and the other Beatles had introduced to the world as the Beatle cut.

Lennon had personal reasons for being apprehensive about the trip to the United States. Prior to leaving London he had announced at a press conference that he and Cynthia had been secretly married. He and Brian Epstein, the Beatles' manager, worried that young American female fans would not buy the Beatles' records after they heard the news that John was a married man with a 10-month-old son, Julian.

Before leaving London for his trip to the United States, Lennon had announced that he and Cynthia Powell had been secretly married and that they had a 10-month-old son.

But their fear that Lennon's marriage would somehow hold the group back from becoming popular was baseless. Sandi Stewart, a 15-year-old who waited for the Beatles to arrive in the United States, remembered how she felt about the Beatles at the time. "When absolutely nothing else in life was good, I'd go to my room and have the Beatles," she said in an interview, "especially my darling John. I got so desperate about him that I wrote a letter to Cynthia. I just told her I was very sorry, but I loved her husband."

Only six months before the Beatles' incredibly swift rise to stardom, the group had played in the tiny confines of the Cavern Club, a basement nightclub in the Beatles' hometown of Liverpool, England. Now they were traveling to America to perform live on the most popular variety show in television history—"The Ed Sullivan Show."

"We all felt a bit sick that first time," Ringo Starr told Hunter Davies, the authorized biographer of the Beatles, in 1967. "We always did, though we never showed it, before anything big. Going to the States was a big step. People said, just because we were popular in England, why should we be [popular in America]?"

But no one needed to have worried about the Beatles' popularity. After their jet landed, the Beatles saw more than 10,000 screaming teenagers crowded into the airport, carrying signs and singing "We Love You Beatles, Oh, Yes We Do." Television, radio, newspaper, and magazine reporters pushed and shoved each other to get close to the illustrious foursome as they stepped from the plane.

Cynthia Lennon found the noise at the airport deafening. "We all thought the screaming was from the jet engines," she later reflected. "But in fact it was the screaming of the fans."

In the airport lounge, the Beatles encountered the biggest press conference they had ever experienced. Some of the New York press corps, aware that the Beatles' appearances in England had created hysteria among their teenaged fans, wondered whether the group would be a bad influence on America's teens.

"Are you a part of a social rebellion against the older generation?" asked one reporter, suspicious of their motives.

"It's a dirty lie," John answered.

"Are you going to get a haircut?" another asked, referring to the controversial long-hair style worn by the four young men.

"We had one yesterday," John replied cheerfully. His quick wit and irreverent sense of humor inspired the other Beatles as they responded to a battery of questions from the media.

"What about the campaign in Detroit to stamp out the Beatles?" a reporter asked.

"We've got a campaign to stamp out Detroit," Paul McCartney retorted.

"What do you do when you're cooped up in your rooms?" yet another queried.

With mock seriousness, George Harrison answered, "We ice skate."

"Do you guys hope to take anything home with you?" another curious reporter asked.

"Yes," they joked, "Rockefeller Center."

The press enjoyed interviewing such quick-witted and amusing celebrities. One of the reporters asked, "What do you think of Beethoven?"

"I love him," Ringo said with a straight face, "especially his poems."

"Was your family in show business?" another reporter inquired of Lennon.

"Well," John replied with a smile, "me dad used to say me mother was a great performer."

Two days later, on Sunday evening, February 9, 1964, the Beatles appeared on "The Ed Sullivan Show," which was televised on the CBS network. Fifty thousand requests for tickets had come in to the theater, which had only 728 seats available, and across the country nearly 74 million people were glued to their TV sets, watching the program. Their appearance on the show held the record for drawing the largest TV audience until 1993.

The Beatles appear with Ed Sullivan (center) during the rehearsal for their February 9, 1964, performance on "The Ed Sullivan Show." Until Michael Jackson's 1993 performance at halftime during Super Bowl XXVII, the Beatles held the record for drawing the largest TV audience ever.

Before introducing the band to the audience, Sullivan read a telegram that he said he had received from Elvis Presley, the nation's most popular rock and roll singer, congratulating the Beatles and wishing them good luck, much to the delight of the screaming fans in the audience. (Years later, the Beatles found out that Elvis did not even like their music and that the telegram had not come from him but from his manager, Colonel Tom Parker, who wanted to get Elvis some free publicity.)

It was later written that during the broadcast of the Beatles' performance on the Sullivan show not a single hubcap was stolen from an automobile or a major crime committed by a teenager in the entire country. If that report was true, it was a very powerful testimony to the appeal of the Beatles and their music.

The day after their appearance on "The Ed Sullivan Show," the Beatles left New York City by train for Washington, D.C. They were booked at the Coliseum for a warm-up concert and then were to return to New

York for two sold-out performances at the world-renowned Carnegie Hall. Twenty thousand fans surrounded the Coliseum's revolving stage while the group played such hits as "Love Me Do," "She Loves You," and "I Want To Hold Your Hand" for the captivated audience.

During the Coliseum concert the Beatles had to endure the first of many painful encounters with well-meaning fans who threw jelly beans at them. "It was terrible," George explained to biographer Hunter Davies. "They hurt. Some newspaper had dug out the old joke, which we'd forgotten about, when John had once said I'd eaten all his jelly babies. Everywhere we went I got them thrown at me."

Despite their discomfort at the concert, the Beatles felt even more uncomfortable later that evening when they had to attend an affair at the British Embassy.

Formal situations had always made Lennon feel especially awkward and ill at ease. An intelligent, sensitive, and rebellious young man, he was deeply aware of the British distinctions between the social classes, and he resented the fact that he would never have been accepted by the upper class of British society had it not been for the Beatles' financial success. George summed up the attitude of the group when he later described official functions to Davies as "always full of snobby people who really loathe our type, but want to see us because we're rich and famous. It's all hypocrisy."

At the British Embassy reception, John, who felt unsure of himself, behaved in his typical manner. "Hello, John," Ambassador Sir David Ormsby-Gore said as he introduced himself to Lennon and the others as they arrived.

"I'm not John," Lennon replied. "I'm Charlie. That's John."

"Hello, John," the ambassador said to George.

"I'm not John, I'm Frank. That's John." George said, pointing to Paul.

"Oh, dear," replied the confused ambassador.

During the evening, the guests at the reception demanded autographs from the Beatles and then became rude when the group grew tired of signing their names. "Look, he can actually write," one man said sarcastically about Lennon, who was signing his name for one of the female guests. John controlled his volatile temper, but when a woman, dressed in an evening gown, cut off a piece of Ringo's hair to take home as a souvenir, John left the reception in disgust. After the embassy fiasco, Brian Epstein promised the group that he would never ask them to attend a diplomatic, royal, or presidential function again.

Throughout the hard times, when the Beatles had struggled to get bookings, Lennon had encouraged the band with a cheer: "To the toppermost of the poppermost!" The Beatles had now risen to the very top of the popular music world. The group's songs had reached number one on the music charts on both sides of the Atlantic Ocean, and it seemed as though only good times lay ahead of them. But Lennon had difficulty coping with the Beatles' success. If he had counted on superstardom to fill his inner needs, he had been greatly mistaken. "The whole Beatle thing was beyond my comprehension," he later admitted as he looked back on those hectic years. "I was eating and drinking like a pig, dissatisfied with myself and subconsciously crying for help."

Lennon was not the only person experiencing turmoil and confusion during the 1960s. Millions of young people had disconnected themselves from their parents' generation in the decade of tumultuous social upheaval.

In the United States, the civil rights movement had successfully demolished the legal basis for segregation— through nonviolent means—and had challenged the practice of racial discrimination in schools, voting booths, criminal courts, public facilities, and housing. But despite this peaceful progress toward racial justice, race riots erupted in the Watts section of Los Angeles, California, in 1965, and 34 people were killed. In 1967, racial violence also exploded in Detroit, Michigan, Newark, New Jersey, and other major cities throughout the South and Northeast.

While the country wrestled with its own social conscience, President John F. Kennedy was assassinated in Dallas, Texas, in 1963, the black nationalist leader Malcolm X was killed in Harlem in New York City in 1965, and in 1968, the civil rights leader Martin Luther King, Jr., and Senator Robert Kennedy fell victim to assassins' bullets in Memphis, Tennessee, and Los Angeles, California, respectively.

Beatlemania swept the world, as this photograph of ardent fans wearing dresses that bear the Beatles' likenesses in Stockholm, Sweden, attests.

Meanwhile, hippies—as long-haired, unconventionally dressed, and rebellious young adults of the counterculture were called—tried to create an alternative life-style to the materialistic world of their parents by rejecting the mores of established society. Moreover, millions of people in this counterculture—including the Beatles—moved away from organized religion in search of their own answers and beliefs.

Society's sexual mores also changed during the 1960s, becoming more relaxed and casual with the influence of such movements as free love, where members of the opposite sex lived openly with one another without marriage.

The field of science also experienced a revolution in the decade with the inspirational triumph of the Apollo 11 astronauts' walk on the moon in 1969. However, the exciting images that the American public saw on their television screens contrasted sharply with the news photos they beheld of the horrific war in Vietnam, where the death toll of American soldiers escalated daily.

The debate about whether the United States should even be fighting in Vietnam quickly spread from college campuses to dining room tables across the country, and it often divided family members as they took sides in the conflict. (For example, in May 1970, the cry for peace in Southeast Asia grew stronger after National Guardsmen tragically killed four students during an antiwar demonstration at Ohio's Kent State University.)

The 1960s had taken a bewildering assortment of directions, including experimentation with "psychedelic" (indicating "mind-altering" or "mind-expanding" properties) drugs, such as LSD (sometimes called acid), psiloybin, and mescaline—all of which produce hallucinogenic effects. The title of psychologist Timothy Leary's film *Turn On, Tune In, and Drop Out* became the motto of the day for the young, who turned to taking drugs and smoking marijuana to "expand [their] consciousness."

In the midst of this decade of turbulence, the Beatles became the most popular musical group in the world. Every record they made shot to the top of the charts, and their evolving musical style and lyrics frequently reflected the social changes that continued to swirl around them. Not only did their music mirror those changes, but in some ways it also influenced them. For example, the song "Lucy in the Sky with Diamonds" had been written by Lennon after inspiration he received from a drawing his young son Julian had shown him. The public, however, took the song to be about an LSD (Lucy, Sky, Diamonds) experience Lennon had had, and consequently, many young fans began to experiment with hallucinogens. People often misunderstood Lennon, and that had frustrated him ever since childhood.

2 "Can't Buy Me Love"

JOHN LENNON'S FATHER, Alfred, whom everyone called Fred, had been raised in an orphanage in Liverpool, England, a large industrial city on the northwest seacoast of Great Britain. Once one of the busiest seaports and manufacturing centers in the world, Liverpool had already begun to decline by the time Fred Lennon became an adult.

In 1930, one week after his 18th birthday, Fred met a flirtatious young woman, Julia Stanley. He later told Hunter Davies what he and Julia had said to each other at their first meeting. "You look silly," Julia had remarked when she saw Fred strolling in a park with a new bowler hat proudly perched on his head.

"You look lovely," young Fred replied, sitting down next to her.

"If you are going to sit next to me," Julia said slyly, "you'll have to take that silly hat off."

Fred got up and promptly threw his new bowler into the lake.

Shortly after their first exchange, Fred and Julia began to date. Julia's parents were not very pleased about their courting—they did not think the

---

Young John Lennon smiles rather mischievously in this childhood photograph. When Lennon was five years old, he had to decide with whom he wished to live—with his father or with his mother. Lennon chose his mother, Julia; however, she took him to her sister Mimi to raise.

The dockyards of Liverpool, England, bustled with activity when John's father, Fred Lennon, first entered the merchant marine as a ship's steward. John Winston Lennon was born in Liverpool on October 9, 1940, during a German bombing raid of the city in World War II.

young man was good enough for their 16-year-old daughter. But the handsome, happy-go-lucky Fred, who became a ship's steward in the merchant marine (the privately or publicly owned commercial ships, such as freight and passenger ships), continued to date Julia whenever he returned to shore. He taught her to play the banjo, and they had lots of fun in each other's company.

After eight years of courtship, Julia and Fred married in December 1938, less than a year before England entered World War II. A week after his wedding, Fred had to ship out to the West Indies and could not return to Liverpool for three months.

Then, on September 3, 1939, Great Britain declared war on Germany after Germany had invaded Poland, England's ally. Because Great Britain is an island, shipments of supplies and military equipment became crucial to its war effort and, consequently, the members of the merchant marine had to make long and dangerous voyages on the high seas.

During one of Fred's short holidays home, in January 1940, Julia became pregnant. On October 9, 1940, while Fred was back at sea, she gave birth to their son, John Winston Lennon, during a heavy bombing raid by the Luftwaffe, the German Air Force. John's middle name, Winston, which he said he never liked, had been given to him in honor of Prime Minister Winston Churchill.

Fred was away for such long periods of time that his young wife became bored and lonely. She began to visit pubs to enjoy the nightlife of dancing and singing. Unable to afford a baby-sitter and too ashamed to ask her sister Mimi to watch her son while she went out to have a good time, Julia, according to Albert Goldman's controversial biography of Lennon entitled *The Lives of John Lennon* (1989), sometimes recklessly left the sleeping child all alone. John, who would awaken to an empty house, cried in the night and occasionally woke the neighbors.

Late in 1943, Fred's paychecks, which he had been sending to Julia, suddenly stopped coming. He had been put in prison in North Africa for smuggling, although he claimed he had been falsely accused and had not been involved in the crime. When he was released in 1944, he found out that Julia was pregnant with another man's child. Baby Victoria was born in June 1945 and given up for adoption. The Lennons tried to patch up their marriage, but by the time Fred returned from another cruise, Julia had fallen in love with Bobby Dykins, a waiter in a local hotel. Fred and Julia separated, and Fred went back to sea.

Julia moved in with Dykins, and they lived together as husband and wife even though they never married. Julia wore her wedding ring and did not correct neighbors when they called her Mrs. Dykins. John, only five years old at the time, was very upset to have this new man living with his mother, and several times he ran away to his Aunt Mimi's. He sometimes took out his feelings of jealousy, frustration, and anger on other children in the neighborhood—his hostile behavior got so out of hand that he was expelled from kindergarten.

Fred Lennon returned to Liverpool in late summer, 1945, and took John for a short holiday along England's southern seacoast. When Julia arrived to take John home, she and Fred fought over who should have custody of the child. Unable to agree on who could best take care of John, they asked the five-year-old boy to decide with whom he wished to live. Torn by the emotional strain of having to make such a momentous decision, John nonetheless chose Julia.

Mary Elizabeth Smith, John's aunt Mimi, holds the ginger cat, called Timothy, that John had once found as a stray. Although Aunt Mimi loved John dearly, she was a strict disciplinarian who tried to bring order to John's life. She often read books to him and encouraged his own appetite for reading.

But Julia did not take John home that day—instead she took him to her sister Mimi to raise. Like other children who have been neglected, uprooted, and forced to choose between mother and father, John developed protective amnesia about this period in his life. "I soon forgot my father," Lennon later said. "It was like he was dead. But I did see my mother now and then, and my feeling never died off for her. I often thought about her, though I never realized that she was living no more than five miles away. Mimi never told me."

So it was at Mimi's house that he received both parental love and discipline, and it was she who filled the role of mother to him. "I used to send him off to bed, panda under one arm, teddy under the other," recalled Mimi years later. "And he sang himself to sleep every night. We so enjoyed having him, they were the best years of my life, bringing him up."

John sometimes asked his aunt about his mother and father. "I didn't want to tell him the details," she admitted to Hunter Davies. "How could I? He was so happy. It would have been wrong to say your father was no good and your mother has found someone else. John was so happy, singing all the time."

Mary Elizabeth, nicknamed Mimi, was Julia's oldest sister and had no children of her own. She and her husband, George Smith, owned a small dairy farm, called Mendips, in the Woolton section of Liverpool. Uncle George was the closest man to a real father John ever knew. He was a natural ally in Mimi's stern household, and he was more tolerant toward the young boy. When John was 10, his uncle George bought him his first musical instrument, a harmonica, which John played incessantly.

Unlike her husband, Mimi was a strict disciplinarian who tried to build a sense of order and routine into a rebellious boy. Her cool, detached personality may not have made her an ideal mother figure, but she and John loved each other very much. "I always think of him as a little boy," she said in 1966. "I know it's stupid. But nothing could compensate for the pleasure he gave me."

"I'd say I had a happy childhood," John told Hunter Davies. "I came out aggressive, but I was never miserable. I was always having a laugh."

Mimi was an avid reader, and she frequently read to John, encouraging his own appetite for books. "His mind was going all the time," she recalled. "It was either drawing, or writing poetry, or reading. He was a great reader. It was always books, books, books." But it was Uncle George who actually had the patience to teach young John how to read and write.

Lennon became fascinated with Lewis Carroll's writings (*Alice's Adventures in Wonderland* and *Through the Looking Glass*), especially the nonsensical poem "Jabberwocky," which begins: "'Twas brillig, and the slithy toves / Did gyre and gimble in the wabe: / All mimsy were the borogoves, / And the mome raths outgrabe." Critics believe Carroll's clever twisting of words and meanings influenced Lennon's own humorous writings, such as *John Lennon in His Own Write* (1964) and *A Spaniard in the Works* (1965).

Lennon also identified with the *Just William* books, popular stories about an English boy who was always out of step with the rest of the world—a boy who just did not fit in. That was how John came to see himself, more and more, as he grew older. "I was different from others then," he painfully reflected in a 1980 interview with David Sheff of *Playboy* magazine. "I was different all my life. What I'm saying, in my insecure way, is 'Nobody seems to understand where I'm coming from. I seem to see things in a different way from most people.' And it's scary when you're a child, because there is nobody to relate to. Neither my auntie nor my friends could ever see it."

What the English school system could see was a very bright young boy, talented in art, who did not apply himself to his studies and one who, along with his best friend, Pete Shotton, was constantly in trouble. Lennon told his aunt Mimi that his lack of interest in school was caused by boring instructors. But there was possibly another reason for his problems: poor eyesight.

At age 11, John was diagnosed as nearsighted and had additional problems with his depth perception. He was too self-conscious to wear the glasses he needed until 1966, when he adopted the horn-rimmed spectacles that he wore in the movie *How I Won the War.* Whatever the reason, Lennon entered Quarry Bank High School in 1951 more concerned with being the class clown than with achieving good grades.

By 1955, Lennon had discovered a different outlet than class cutup for his rough-hewn creative energy: rock and roll music. Pete Shotton recalled that he and John often listened to a late-night Radio Luxembourg show, broadcast from Belgium, that was devoted to the latest American records. "Rock Around the Clock" by Bill Haley and the Comets and Elvis Presley's hits, such as "Heartbreak Hotel" and "Blue Suede Shoes," were some of the boys' favorites. John was so excited about music that he pestered his aunt Mimi until she finally bought him an inexpensive guitar.

In June 1955, Lennon's only male role model and his most reliable family ally, Uncle George, died unexpectedly while John was visiting another aunt in Scotland. "When he got back," Mimi remembered, "I said, 'John, Uncle George is dead.' He went deathly white and went upstairs and said nothing. He never mentioned it again."

Almost as suddenly as his uncle had left him, Lennon's mother reentered his life. Julia was an attractive woman, five feet two inches tall, with shoulder-length brown hair and a charming personality. According to John's half sister Julia Dykins Baird, her mother had an infectious, optimistic outlook on life and was always full of lighthearted fun. Hungry for affection, 15-year-old Lennon found Julia a much less demanding mother than Mimi was.

Thrilled by his mother's renewed attention, John visited her house frequently to get to know his two younger half sisters, Julia and Jacqueline, and to use her house as

On February 6, 1957, rock and roll legend Bill Haley (center) and his Comets rehearse at the Dominique Theatre in London, where they opened their British tour. As a teenager, Lennon was a devoted fan of Haley's.

a refuge from school or as an escape from Mimi's supervision. While John stayed there, Julia taught him to play
his guitar using the banjo chords that Fred had shown
her. John and his friend Pete often listened to her large
record collection of popular music. John enjoyed a sense

Rock and roll "king" Elvis Presley, arms outstretched, sways rhythmically from side to side while singing in 1956. Lennon listened eagerly to Presley's hit songs, such as "Heartbreak Hotel" and "Blue Suede Shoes," when they were broadcast from Belgium on a Radio Luxembourg show.

of freedom from responsibility at Julia's, an ambience he was unable to experience in his own home.

Julia's free spirit—a trait that could be considered undesirable when it came to raising young children—allowed John the opportunity to "be himself" without having to worry about what adults might think about him. Frequently, however, Julia acted more like an indulgent aunt than a responsible mother. Unlike Mimi, she did not seem to mind when John skipped school. Instead of being annoyed, Julia used to say to John, "Don't worry about school, don't worry about a thing. Everything's going to work out fine."

But things did not work out fine for Julia and John. On July 15, 1958, while 17-year-old John waited for Julia at her house, she was struck and killed by a speeding car. Only moments before the accident, Julia and Mimi had stood talking by the garden gate in front of Mimi's house on Menlove Avenue, where John had lived with his aunt for 12 years.

When the police came to inform the Dykins family of Julia's death, John took it very hard. "We were sitting waiting for her to come home, wondering why she was so late," he remembered bitterly. "The copper [policeman] came to the door to tell us about the accident. It was just as it is supposed to be, the way it is in the films, asking if I was her son and all. Then he told us [John and his stepfather] and we both went white. It was the worst-ever thing that happened to me. We had caught up so much, me and Julia, in just a few years."

Dazed and in anguish, John and his stepfather rushed to the hospital. When they arrived, John could not bring himself to go in and see his mother's body. Instead, he returned to Mimi's house alone, where, according to a neighbor, he sat on the front porch and played his guitar.

"I lost my mother twice," he said, painfully, later. "Once when I moved in with my auntie, and once again when I was reestablishing my relationship with her. That was a really hard time for me—very traumatic. And it just absolutely made me very, very bitter."

Before his mother had been killed, John was just coming to grips with the confusing relationships in his family—relationships that had been complicated to begin with. "We were well into our teens before we finally unravelled the complexities for ourselves," John's half sister, Julia Dykins Baird later wrote in her book *John Lennon, My Brother* (1988). "We were never told anything. The children in our family were always protected from any truth."

3 ★ The Birth of the Beatles

MIMI WATCHED IN EXASPERATION as young Lennon practiced hour after hour on the little guitar she had bought him. "The guitar's all very well, John," she had told him many times. "But you'll never make a living out of it."

Nevertheless, that was exactly why he was practicing. He had formed a musical group with his friends, Pete Shotton, Nigel Whalley, and Ivan Vaughan, and had called it the Quarry Men, after the high school they attended, Quarry Bank. By all accounts they were not very accomplished musicians, but it did not matter because a country-and-western style, easy-to-play kind of music called skiffle had become the rage at local parties. Skiffle bands generally featured a washboard (for its scraping sound), a bass fiddle, which was usually made from a washtub, and guitars. The Quarry Men were scheduled to play two sets at a St. Peter's Parish Church fete on Saturday afternoon, July 6, 1957.

According to Pete Shotton, who described the event in his 1983 biography, *John Lennon in My Life*, while the band set up for its second show, Ivan

---

Beatle Lennon plays a composition on his guitar. Lennon played the banjo chords that his mother had taught him on the guitar until he learned the proper guitar chords from Paul McCartney, whom he had met in 1957 at one of the Quarry Men's performances.

introduced John to his baby-faced, guitar-carrying friend Paul McCartney. At their first encounter, Lennon was very wary of McCartney, who was two years younger than he was and obviously talented. Paul was equally cool and reserved toward John. But the awkwardness between them disappeared when Paul took out his guitar and played some songs.

Paul began with "Twenty Flight Rock," a song that the Quarry Men had found too difficult to play. Paul also showed John the proper guitar chords to play rather than the banjo chords that he had learned from his mother.

"Well, Pete," John said to Shotton after Paul had left, "what did you think of him?"

"I like him," Shotton replied.

"So what would you think about having Paul in the group?" John asked.

"It's okay with me," responded Pete, "if you want him in."

John had realized that Paul was at least as good a guitar player as he was. "I'd been king-pin up to then," Lennon later admitted, "'now,' I thought, 'if I take him on, what will happen?'"

After Paul helped John master guitar chords, the two began to dabble in songwriting. One of John's first efforts, "One After 909," later appeared on the Beatles' final album, *Let It Be* (1970). Because John and Paul's musical talents complemented one another they agreed to credit all their work jointly as Lennon and McCartney songs, regardless of who actually wrote the piece. (Nearly all of John and Paul's work of this period was accidentally thrown out years later by one of Paul's girlfriends during a spring cleaning of Paul's house in London.)

After Paul and John played together at several local engagements, Paul told John about another musician he knew, 14-year-old George Harrison, who could play the guitar even better than Paul could. Not only could he play chords, but he could play solos using individual notes. Although John was impressed by George's talent when he heard him audition for the band, John was not keen on having someone as young as George in the group. However, after several weeks, George finally persuaded John into accepting him as a member of the band.

By 1958, Lennon had grown into a tall, lanky young man. He wore pants that were extremely tight, and he combed his hair in a long, greasy wave over his forehead, imitating Elvis Presley. But that summer his mother had been killed, and he took her death very hard. It made matters worse that he was not getting along with his aunt, and he later admitted to an interviewer that he developed a tough, rebellious attitude to hide his unhappiness.

The year before, in 1957, he had enrolled in Liverpool Art College, despite having failed his "O" levels—the British equivalent to the Scholastic Aptitude Tests (SATs) given in the United States. He was accepted into the college on a recommendation from a sympathetic headmaster at Quarry Bank, who had recognized John's artistic ability.

Lennon did little or no schoolwork, and it seemed to Cynthia Powell, the pretty young woman sitting behind him in lettering class, that every other word out of his mouth was a curse. She complained that his breath smelled of beer and that he chain-smoked cigarettes given to him by classmates who were too frightened by his tough manner to refuse him.

Cynthia seemed to be the opposite of John. She came from a proper middle-class family, dressed conservatively, and had blond hair, pale skin, and large blue eyes. She thought Lennon was a vulgar and ill-mannered bully.

After his mother's death, John had begun to drink alcohol heavily. Sometimes he and Pete Shotton attended late-night clubs, where Lennon lashed out at anyone who rubbed him the wrong way. Friends from the art college have told interviewers that, when sober, John was charming, witty, and funny; but when drunk, he could be very offensive.

One fall afternoon, however, Cynthia heard him play his guitar and sing "Ain't She Sweet" in the school's basement dining hall. This was not the John she thought she knew, the boy who could be hurtful and mean and who had a sharp tongue and short temper. Gone from his face was the cruel look that had been so full of anger and malice. Instead, she saw a tender, vulnerable, and lonely young man. "I wanted desperately to see him at peace with himself and the world," she explained in 1983 in *The Love You Make*, written by Peter Brown and Steven Gaines. It was then, she said, that she fell head over heels in love with him.

To attract Lennon's attention, Cynthia changed her hairstyle and her way of dressing to imitate Brigitte Bardot, a French movie star whom she had heard John had a crush on. Later that year, after a college Christmas party, John invited Cynthia to a local pub that was crowded with rowdy students celebrating the end of the semester. That evening, John and Cynthia stayed together in a college friend's one-room apartment.

Lennon was able to get through the difficult period following his mother's death with help from Cynthia and his friend Stuart Sutcliffe, called Stu, who was a promising art student and who many thought looked like the American movie star James Dean. Lennon included Stu, whom he thought was artistically gifted, in his small circle of friends. "I always had a gang," Lennon said in his 1980 interview with David Sheff, "a group of four or five guys around me who would play various roles in my life, [both] supportive and subservient." When Sutcliffe sold one of his paintings for the sum of 60 pounds sterling, John talked him into buying a bass guitar—not because he could play it but because John wanted him in the group.

Stuart Sutcliffe, called Stu, studied art at the Liverpool Art College, where he and Lennon first met. Stu became a member of Lennon's band after Lennon urged him to buy a bass guitar with the money Stu had made from the sale of one of his paintings. In 1962, Stu died from a brain tumor, probably as a result of the beating he had been given by thugs after the chaotic Litherland Town Hall performance.

In the fall of 1958, the band added Pete Best, the owner of a new set of drums, and attracted much attention on the Liverpool nightclub scene. The group (now comprised of John, Paul, George, Pete, and Stu) struggled financially through 1959 and often had to perform in the rough "cellar clubs," the basement clubs near the dockyards. It was not glamorous work.

During this period, the band had played under various names, including Johnny and the Moondogs, but none of them pleased Lennon very much. He searched for a better name to fit their new look of black leather jackets and tight trousers. Because he liked the sound of an

American group called the Crickets, he thought of calling the group the Beetles, but enjoying puns, he decided on the spelling "Beatles," which also referred to the style of music played by the "beat groups" of Liverpool.

Finally, in the early summer of 1960, the group got a job outside Liverpool playing as backup band for Johnny Gentle, a small-time singer. They called themselves the Silver Beatles for this tour only and played run-down halls in small towns in Scotland. With this minor success behind them, their tour arranger, Allan Williams, booked them for a six-week nightclub engagement in Hamburg, West Germany (now Germany).

What they hoped would be their big break turned out to be hardly a step up from the Liverpool docks. The port city of Hamburg, on the Elbe River, not far from the North Sea, was a shipping center. The Reeperbahn, the main street of the city's red-light district (where there were numerous houses of prostitution), was famous for its strip clubs and legal brothels. Gangsters and hoodlums frequented the nightclubs, and gang warfare sometimes broke out among the criminal element. The nightclub owners of Hamburg hired waiters for their muscle and brawn rather than for their ability to wait on tables.

The Beatles were employed to play at the Indra Club, a dreary little place with an elephant-shaped neon sign out front. The owner of the club expected them to play from 7:00 P.M. until 3:00 A.M. and sometimes seven days a week.

When the Beatles appeared on the tiny stage—instead of the usual girlie show—the German audience not only wanted to listen to music but wanted to be entertained as well. The club's owner told the band to "*Mach Schau*" (make show) and demanded that they jump around and perform rather than just play their guitars and sing.

Lennon realized that the Beatles had to change their act in order to keep the job. Consequently, while the band stamped out the rhythm on the wooden floor, he did imitations of people and taunted the audience while he sang. The drunken crowd delighted in his antics. "We played very loud in Hamburg," he told Hunter Davies. "Bang, bang all the time. The Germans loved it."

One of the more difficult problems the Beatles had to solve was how to play the small number of songs they knew and still entertain the crowd. "Back home in Liverpool, we'd only ever done hour-long sessions," Lennon told Davies. "In Hamburg we had to play for eight hours, so we really had to find a new way of playing." They filled some of the time with their own musical compositions—getting a chance to try out and improve their songwriting skills—while the rest of the time they simply played each song longer.

With the exception of Pete Best, who seemed able to resist the temptation of the wild life in Hamburg, the band members used German diet pills to help keep up their energy. And because they could drink beer at no cost, they got drunk nearly every night. "We got drunk a lot," Lennon admitted to Davies. "They [the audience] would be sending us drinks up all the time, so we drank too much."

John was only 20 years old at the time the Beatles played in Hamburg, and George was barely 17. Without parental supervision, they found it hard to resist the lure of drugs, alcohol, and sex. "We soon realized [young women] were easy to get," Lennon recalled. "We had a lot of girls."

Instead of burning out from the effects of late nights and liquor, the Beatles became a powerhouse show band onstage. They became so popular that the Indra Club had to close after two months because the neighbors complained of the noise. The band moved their show to the Kaiserkeller, a much larger hall, after their contract was extended for five more months. By then the Beatles knew how to *Mach Schau* and drew bigger and bigger crowds.

Despite his carousing, Lennon wrote long, touching love letters home to Cynthia. In some of his letters he mentioned Astrid Kirchherr and her roommate, Klaus Voorman. Astrid, an exotic-looking woman who dressed in all-black clothes, had sad, dark eyes that peeked out from a pixie haircut. Klaus had introduced Astrid to the

After Stu's departure from the group in March 1961, the four remaining Beatles, guitarists John Lennon, George Harrison, and Paul McCartney and drummer Pete Best, recorded their first song, "My Bonnie Lies Over the Ocean," playing as backup to the singer Tony Sheridan in April 1961.

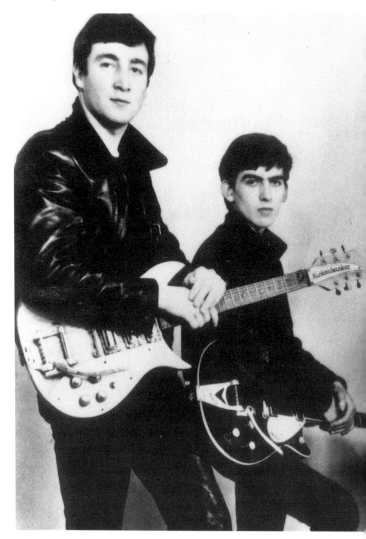

band after he had heard them play at the Kaiserkeller. Astrid, in turn, invited other German art students to hear the Beatles, and soon the nightclub became the in place to be for young intellectuals and artists in Hamburg.

Astrid and another friend, Jürgen Vollmer, photographed the Beatles often, and their pictures later became popular images of the Beatles' early days. Astrid designed and cut—with the exception of Pete's—the combed-

forward, bowl-shaped hairstyle that became the Beatles' trademark. Despite the language barrier between Stu and Astrid, Astrid recognized Stu's sensitive and artistic soul and fell deeply in love with him. In early November 1960, only two months after they met, Astrid and Stu were engaged to be married.

Fate intervened, however, when the Hamburg police discovered that George was not yet 18—and therefore too young to work in West Germany—and deported him back to England. At the end of November the other Beatles, including Stu, each straggled home, one by one, cold and broke. John arrived at Menlove Avenue in the middle of the night. "Where's your 100 pounds a night?" Mimi asked John, referring to the lie John had told her about how much money he would make in Germany to get her permission to go there.

"Just like you, Mimi," answered John on the way up to his bedroom, "to go on about money when you know I'm tired."

According to Davies, John stayed in bed for two weeks, depressed about his return to Mendips. When the band finally played together again, they appeared at the Casbah Club, a small coffee club owned by Pete Best's mother. But they were not the same tame group that had played there many times before. Hamburg had changed them; they were now seasoned professional performers, full of confidence and stage presence—and they looked like no one else in Liverpool. They wore cowboy boots, denim jackets, leather pants, and a new hairstyle combed over their foreheads. Word spread quickly about the new, improved Beatles, and within weeks they played shows at the larger Cavern Club on Mathew Street. This dark, damp cellar club, formerly a jazz club, was not a particularly attractive place, having once been a warehouse, but it became a very popular spot with Liverpool's young music fans. Beat music—loud music played on amplified guitars and drums—found a home in the Cavern Club.

Perhaps the most important engagement after the Beatles' return from Hamburg occurred at the Litherland Town Hall dance on December 27, 1960. The performance so electrified the audience that a riot erupted among the rowdy revelers in attendance, many of whom were hurt during the chaos. Trapped by some thugs after the show, Stu, who was slightly built, was badly beaten before Lennon and Best could come to his rescue.

On February 25, 1961, George turned 18, and the band returned to Hamburg to work at the Top Ten Club. Stu and Astrid were reunited. When Cynthia came to visit Lennon during her spring break, she thought Astrid and Stu looked like twins. They wore matching clothes and hairstyles and even ordered the same food in restaurants. But as Stu grew closer to Astrid, he grew further away from the band. Even John, usually a staunch ally, joined Paul and ridiculed Stu's mediocre bass playing.

Usually quiet and shy, Stu had suddenly become moody and occasionally hostile. He began to suffer headaches so painful that he would bang his head against the wall. His unpredictable behavior—sometimes he was happy and other times depressed—caused friction between him and the other band members. In March 1961, Stu decided to leave the group to marry Astrid and stay in West Germany to continue his art career.

In April, the four remaining Beatles recorded their first song in a Hamburg auditorium. The Beat Boys, as the producer insisted they be called, played backup to a moderately successful singer, Tony Sheridan, on the single "My Bonnie Lies Over the Ocean." It would be this obscure recording that would bring the Beatles to the attention of the man who would help make them superstars.

"To the Toppermost of the Poppermost"

N SATURDAY, OCTOBER 28, 1961, a few months after the Beatles' return from Hamburg, Raymond Jones, a young man wearing a leather jacket, walked into one of the North End Music Stores (NEMS) record shops in central Liverpool.

"There is a record I want," Jones said to the store manager, Brian Epstein. "It's called 'My Bonnie' and it was made in Germany. Have you got it?"

"Who is it by?" asked Epstein, who was an efficient and highly organized businessman.

"You won't have heard of them," Jones replied, "it's by a group called the Beatles."

Epstein, who prided himself on never turning away a customer's request, said he would look into getting a copy. When two other teenagers came by the following day with the same request, Epstein discovered that the group

---

Crowds await the arrival of Princess Margaret at the royal premiere of the Beatles' first movie, *A Hard Day's Night,* at the London Pavilion in 1964.

they had asked about was not German, as he had first thought, but British, and played regularly at the Cavern Club nearby.

Epstein, a 27-year-old bachelor with brown hair, fair skin, and handsome features, lived at home with his parents in the Childwall suburb of Liverpool. He had managed a record section in his well-to-do Jewish family's chain of successful furniture stores, but after sales mounted in 1959 the Epsteins opened the NEMS record store, under Brian's management, in the center of Liverpool's shopping district.

Two days after Jones and the other teenagers had come into NEMS searching for the Beatles' record, Brian decided to hear what had excited the young record buyers. Impeccably dressed in a suit and tie, Epstein descended into the stale, smoky, crowded confines of the Cavern Club to hear the Beatles perform.

Beneath street level, the club's three arched brick tunnels formed a subterranean dance hall where at least 200 young adults crammed together to dance and listen to the Beatles. The Beatles wore tight leather pants and black jackets and played raw, high-energy rock and roll music on a tiny stage. In Epstein's autobiography, *A Cellar Full of Noise*, published in 1964, he said that their driving rock and roll sound and onstage enthusiasm that night fascinated him:

> They were not very tidy and not very clean. But they were tidier and cleaner than anyone else who performed at that lunch-time session or, for that matter, at most of the sessions I later attended. I had never seen anything like the Beatles on any stage. They smoked as they played and they ate and talked and pretended to hit each other. They turned their backs on the audience and shouted at them and laughed at private jokes.

After the Beatles had finished playing, the Cavern disc jockey, having recognized him in the crowd, announced over the loudspeaker that Brian Epstein was in the audience. Epstein, embarrassed by the announcement, made his way toward the stage to speak to the Beatles. When he reached the group, he told them he was interested in hearing their German disc "My Bonnie." The Beatles looked pleased and led Epstein into the small band room next to the stage, where they played the record for him. Epstein liked the record and stayed at the Cavern Club to hear the second half of the Beatles' program. Epstein commented on the experience in his autobiography, "I . . . found myself liking the Beatles more and more. There was some indefinable charm there. They were extremely amusing and in a rough 'take it or leave it way' very attractive." Several days later, Epstein convinced the group to allow him to be their manager.

"I suppose it was all part of being bored with simply selling records," Epstein later told Hunter Davies. "The Beatles . . . were also getting bored with Liverpool. They wanted to do something new."

Immediately Epstein used his influence as a record retailer to arrange an audition for the Beatles with Decca Records. On New Year's Eve, 1961, Neil Aspinall, Pete Best's friend, who became the Beatles road manager for the remainder of their career, drove the nervous band in his unheated van to London.

The Beatles had recorded "My Bonnie" in an old auditorium. But the Decca audition took place in a professional studio, where several anonymous men sat behind a glass control-booth window. The audition did not go well. The strange surroundings and a fit of nerves took away the energy and spontaneity that distinguished the Beatles whenever they performed onstage. They recorded 14 songs, but only 3 were Lennon and McCartney originals: "Like Dreamers Do," "Hello, Little Girl," and "Love of the Loved." According to Peter Brown and Steven Gaines in *The Love You Make*, published in 1983, their stiff, lifeless performance—especially Pete's drumming—sounded terrible on the old standards, such as "Red Sails in the Sunset," "The Sheik of Araby," and "Besame Mucho," that Brian had insisted they play.

Decca turned them down because, as one official told Brian, "Not to mince words, Mr. Epstein, we don't like your boys' sound. Groups of four guitarists are on the way out." John became furious, believing that Epstein had ruined their recording chances by making them play old songs. It was the first, but not the last, time John felt that he had to compromise himself in order to make it big in the music world.

Discouraged by their lack of progress in England, the group returned to Hamburg on April 13, 1962, to play at the Star Club, the Reeperbahn's newest and biggest nightclub. Astrid, dressed as always in black, met the Beatles at the airport.

"Where is Stu?" they shouted when they saw her standing alone without her husband.

Astrid choked on her words, "Stu is dead."

The band was grief stricken. John and Stu had been writing to each other, and when John heard the news he broke down in tears. Stu had collapsed and died in Astrid's arms only the day before. Later they learned that there had been a small tumor on his brain caused by a traumatic depression of the skull. Doctors thought it could have been caused by a sharp blow to his head—possibly from the beating that John and Pete had rescued Stu from less than a year and a half earlier.

The shock of Stu's death and the guilt Lennon felt over the way he had treated Stu before he had left the group sent Lennon deep into the netherworld of Hamburg's nightlife. He drowned his sorrow in liquor and showed little regard for his public behavior, which became increasingly outrageous.

Meanwhile, by the end of May Brian Epstein had convinced Parlophone, a small division of EMI records, to let the group audition. CONGRATULATIONS BOYS, his telegram to Germany read, EMI REQUESTS RECORDING SESSION. PLEASE REHEARSE NEW MATERIAL.

On June 6, 1962, the excited band members arrived at EMI's studios, located in an imposing mansion on Abbey Road, in St. John's Wood, London. They felt more comfortable with Parlophone's producer, George Martin, than they had with the producers at Decca Records.

"Let me know if there is anything you don't like," Martin said, according to Davies, before they began.

"Well, for a start," replied a smiling George Harrison, "I don't like your tie."

This time they discarded the old standards in favor of their own compositions, such as "Love Me Do." At the end of the session, however, Martin would not commit to a record contract. It was obvious to him that Pete's dull, heavy drumming did not sound as good in a recording studio as it did in a cavernous beer hall. Pete Best did not know it then, but his days as a Beatle were numbered.

Early in August 1962, George Martin offered a record contract to Epstein and the Beatles. He recognized, from the audition tapes, that the band members had a special, driving quality to their music and that, although the drumming was not really good enough, they showed much promise. On August 16, Pete Best, who had not been told about the record contract, went to the NEMS office at Epstein's behest.

After making nervous small talk, Epstein got down to the business the band had insisted he attend to as their manager. "The boys want you out and Ringo in," Epstein blurted out embarrassingly. Ringo Starr, a 22-year-old drummer, had also played in Hamburg in one of Liverpool's other bands, Rory Storme and the Hurricanes.

On August 4, 1963, the Beatles receive a silver disc for the 250,000-plus sales of their hit single "Please Please Me." Joining them in their acceptance of the award is their Parlophone record producer, George Martin, who stands between Ringo Starr and Lennon.

"Why?" asked the stunned Pete Best, who later wrote about the meeting in his autobiography.

"They don't think you're a good enough drummer, Pete," Brian explained, "and George Martin doesn't think you're good enough either."

"I am as good, if not better, than Ringo," Best replied, unable to understand why he was being expelled from the group after all this time.

Pete Best had built up a loyal following in Liverpool, and when the local fans found out about his ouster, they were upset by it—they felt it was a dirty trick. But the change had been made, and the Beatles officially became

John, Paul, George, and Ringo. (In the following two years the Beatles earned approximately $40 million, whereas Pete Best, who became a baker, earned about $2,496.)

John, too, received some shocking news in August—his girlfriend, Cynthia, was pregnant. "There's only one thing for it, Cyn," John had said, according to Goldman, when Cynthia tearfully told him her news, "we'll have to get married."

In the presence of Paul McCartney, George Harrison, Brian Epstein, and some of Cynthia's relatives, John Lennon and Cynthia Powell were married on August 23,

1962, in the Mount Pleasant Registry Office in Liverpool.

Believing the news of Lennon's marriage and impending fatherhood would hurt the band's chances of success, Epstein insisted that Cynthia stay at home and not accompany John to his performances around England. In Solt and Eagan's book *Imagine*, Cynthia described her wifely duties as: "Steer clear of the press, keep out of the way, and 'I love you regardless.'"

The Beatles' constant concert schedule helped their first three singles—"Love Me Do" (released in October 1962), "Please Please Me" (released in January 1963), and "From Me to You" (released in April 1963)—slowly climb the charts in Great Britain. As a result of the busy schedule, John and Cynthia saw very little of each other during Cynthia's pregnancy, but by moving in with John's aunt at Mendips, Cynthia was able to patch up the bad feelings that had developed between Mimi and John.

John and Cynthia's son, John Charles Julian Lennon, whom they called Julian, was born at Sefton General Hospital in Liverpool, on April 8, 1963, while John was away on tour. He arrived several days later and was thrilled over the sight of the tiny boy who looked just like him. "He's bloody marvelous, isn't he, Cyn?" Cynthia remembered him saying while he held his baby for the first time. But Cynthia's joy at seeing her husband cradle their son in his arms faded when he informed her he was taking a break from his grinding tour schedule to go on a vacation to Spain—with Brian Epstein.

"How could you go off and leave us like that?" she demanded. "And with Brian, no less."

As noted in Brown and Gaines's *The Love You Make*, Lennon responded defensively, "Being bloody selfish again? I've been working . . . on one-night stands for months now. I deserve a vacation. Anyway, Brian wants me to go, and I owe it to the poor guy. Who else does he have to go away with?"

Cynthia's annoyance at John for taking a holiday at this time was aggravated by the fact that he was going with Brian Epstein. It was obvious to many people close to the Beatles that Brian, a homosexual who never publicly admitted to being gay, was attracted to John. English society at the time, especially working-class Liverpool, was intolerant of homosexuals. In fact, Brian had been beaten up on several occasions by people who were offended by his sexual orientation. After Brian and John returned from Spain, John had to contend with a lot of teasing and suggestive remarks. John emphatically denied that he had a homosexual encounter with Brian—even to the point of breaking the collarbone and three ribs of an old friend in a fight that followed the friend's teasing. John later admitted to Peter Brown, however, that he had allowed Brian to touch him. "[I was] thinking like a writer, all the time . . . 'I am experiencing this,'" he told Brown.

During the summer of 1963, the Beatles' career steamrolled faster and faster as their heavy concert schedule spread Beatlemania throughout Great Britain. Back in London in August, they recorded their fourth single, "She Loves You," which immediately rose to number one on the charts. Shortly thereafter, while on tour in Sweden, they heard that they had been invited to play in England's biggest, most prestigious show of the year—the Royal Variety Show at the Prince of Wales Theatre in London for Queen Elizabeth II and her family.

At the performance the Beatles sang "She Loves You," "Till There Was You," and "Twist and Shout" and became the hit of the nationally televised show. With the queen mother, Princess Margaret, and Lord Snowdon seated in the balcony, John tried to get the concert hall's audience involved in the band's music. "Will the people in the cheaper seats clap your hands," he exhorted, according to Brown. "The rest of you," he continued, looking up at the royal box, "can just rattle your jewelry."

After the Royal Variety Show, the Beatles became the talk of the entire country. Television, newspaper, and magazine reporters hounded the Beatles, and British manufacturers besieged Epstein with requests to use the *Beatles* name in advertising their various products. On December 29, 1963, when the music reviewer of the respected London *Sunday Times* called Lennon and McCartney "the greatest composers since Beethoven," Brian Epstein knew it was time to see how America would react to the Beatles' music. He immediately flew to New York and made arrangements for their appearance on "The Ed Sullivan Show."

Because of the recent assassination of President John F. Kennedy, many of the still-mourning American public desperately looked for something or someone to take their minds off the horrible tragedy. For the Beatles, the

The Beatles clown around on stage at one of their concerts in 1963. The Beatles' manager, Brian Epstein, had helped make the Beatles popular by organizing their schedules, toning down their rough behavior, and persuading them to wear suits while performing. Although money came pouring in, Epstein's poor business deals eventually cost the Beatles hundreds of millions of dollars.

timing of their arrival in the United States could not have been better; their upbeat brand of music caught the attention of an entire generation of Americans.

When the band returned to England from their successful debut in the United States, Lennon had little time for his family. The Beatles' first movie, *A Hard Day's Night*, began production in March 1964. In the movie, the four boys play themselves but keep getting into trouble as a result of the antics of Paul's fictitious grandfather. Movie critics as well as the public loved what today can be called the forerunner of the music video. *A Hard Day's Night*, which cost only $600,000 to make and grossed $4.5 million in its first year, remains one of the most lucrative box-office hits ever filmed—in comparison to its total cost to produce—in movie history.

"This is going to surprise you," wrote one critic in the *New York Times*, "but the new film, with those incredible chaps, is a whale of a comedy." In *Show* magazine, Arthur Schlesinger, Jr., called *A Hard Day's Night* "a smart and stylish film, exhilarating in its audacity and modernity." However, the group was so preoccupied with their newfound fame as movie stars that not one of the Beatles looked closely at their financial contracts.

According to several sources, including Peter Brown, who was closest to Brian Epstein in arranging the Beatles' business matters, Epstein had already made a series of financial blunders in managing the band. He had signed many contracts with novelty marketers and licensees to use the Beatles name for too little money and on too generous terms. Even the Beatles' music publisher, Northern Songs, and their record company, Parlophone/EMI, received more money than the Beatles did for their songs. Although the Beatles earned more money than they had ever dreamed possible, other companies raked in much more money than they did from their own record sales.

The movie deal with United Artists, for example, offered the Beatles about $75,000 altogether for their appearance in the film, plus a percentage of the profits. This was a relatively small advance, but the producers were willing to be more generous with the percentage of profits they would agree to give the Beatles—as high as 25 percent. According to Brown, when the film producers and Epstein began to discuss actual numbers, Epstein thought for a moment and said, "I won't accept anything less than 7.5 per cent." To make a bad business deal worse, he agreed to a contract of three movies that allowed the rights to each film to revert to the film's producer after 15 years.

In Epstein's defense, one must say that everything happened so quickly and that no one could have predicted how incredibly successful the Beatles would ultimately become. Furthermore, Brian's contribution to the success of the Beatles' early career was crucial. He had persisted in getting them recorded, and his influence had toned down their rough ways. He organized their schedules, insisted on more refined behavior onstage and in public, and encouraged them to wear suits while performing. Epstein's tireless efforts effectively helped them break into the big time and earn millions of dollars. But some of his poor business judgments eventually also cost the Beatles hundreds of millions of dollars.

With the Beatles' new wealth pouring in, Lennon decided to spend his share of the profits on a place to hide away from his hysterical fans. In July 1964, he purchased a mansion, called Kenwood, on an estate in Weybridge, England, and moved there with Cynthia and Julian.

Only a few miles away, Fred Lennon pushed his arms deeper into the hot dishwater of a hotel's kitchen sink. According to Hunter Davies, another worker, who sat reading the local newspaper while Fred Lennon toiled through the dishes, came upon a photo of the Beatles returning from their appearance in the United States. She peered closely at the photo and was struck by the resemblance between John Lennon, Beatle, and Fred Lennon, dishwasher.

"If that is not your son, Freddy," she said, pointing out John's photo to him, "then I don't know what."

When Fred realized that John was his son, he sold his story to the *Daily Express* newspaper. "I'd like John to see what sort of bloke I really am," Fred said in the interview. Then he made it clear he would not decline any financial help "if John happened to offer it."

Lennon had contradictory emotions about meeting his father, a small, dapper-looking man with a square face and thinning gray hair. John still resented his abandonment as a child, yet he was excited about gaining a family member he thought he had lost nearly 20 years earlier.

Lennon agreed to see his father, and their first meeting went fairly well, considering the awkward circumstances. "He's good news," John told Pete Shotton the next day. "A real funny guy—a loony just like me."

But too much time had passed for the father and son—Fred had nothing left to offer John. During those long years apart, Fred had become an alcoholic. Despite receiving a monthly allowance from his son, Fred Lennon soon exploited the relationship by selling his story to anyone who would pay him. He released a record called "That's My Life" in 1965, then married, with much publicity, a young university student who had worked as a baby-sitter for Julian and as a secretary for Cynthia. John's patience with his father finally wore thin after Fred, who had had too much to drink, allegedly tried to seduce Cynthia and then asked John for a loan. John cut off his father's allowance and refused to see him again. Fred did not reenter John's life until 1976, when John telephoned him shortly before Fred died of cancer in a charity ward in Brighton, England.

5 "Help!"

THE BEATLES' SUMMER TOUR of 1964 began in Europe, then continued on to Canada, the United States, Hong Kong, Australia, and New Zealand. Attendance at the concerts broke all records, but the largest single turnout was at the concert in Adelaide, Australia, in June. More than 300,000 fans mobbed the streets to catch a glimpse of the Beatles as they drove by. Lennon and McCartney songs held the top five spots on the record charts on three continents—all within the same time period—a milestone that to this day has not come close to being broken.

Although Paul, George, and Ringo enjoyed the adulation of their fans, John took his fame uneasily. Because they were under intense public scrutiny, John and the other Beatles allowed Brian Epstein to manage their public lives. Lennon, who always felt rebellious when asked to conform, was at odds with himself. Like many people who had become famous in their youth, it became apparent to him that stardom—because of the personal sacrifices required to achieve it—offered him hollow satisfaction.

The Beatles appear in a scene from the movie *Help!*, which was released in 1965. Lennon, who was now rich, famous, and living in a mansion, did not handle his fame well. He became very unhappy, believing he had been trapped into playing the role that the public expected of him.

Lennon, however, enjoyed writing, and his book of puns and cartoon doodles entitled *John Lennon in His Own Write*, published by Simon & Schuster, rushed to the top of the best-seller list in 1964. One of Lennon's doodles includes a dog who stands in a wrestling ring before a crowded arena of onlookers. Called "The Wrestling Dog" the story begins, "One upon a tom in a far off distant land far across the sea miles away from anyway over the hills as the crow barks 39 peoble lived miles away from anywhere on a little island on a distant land." More than 300,000 copies of the book were sold in Great Britain alone.

Lennon was quite surprised that many literary critics, who should have known better, took his most inane comments as deep insight. In *The Love You Make*, Brown and Gaines relate an example of Lennon's frustration over being misunderstood. After a nightlong celebration, John, still feeling the effects a hangover, and Cynthia attended a luncheon held in Lennon's honor at a literary society.

Someone at the luncheon asked him, "Do you make conscious use of onomatopoeia?" (Onomatopoeia is the formation of words that imitate sounds, such as *buzz*, *hiss*, and *sizzle*.)

"Automatic pier?" John dazedly replied from behind dark glasses. "I don't know what you're talking about," he added.

When it was time to make a speech before the literary society, he tottered to the microphone and mumbled softly, "Thank you very much," and then sat down.

"What did he say?" a perplexed member of the audience asked aloud.

Another guest replied, "He said, 'You've got a lucky face.'"

Many in the audience gave him a big round of applause and were in awe of what they thought was his obscure witticism. Lennon did not appreciate people idolizing him in this way—the absurdity of the situation only reinforced Lennon's insecurities about himself and about everyone's misconception of him.

In June 1965, Lennon had his second book of puns and cartoons, *A Spaniard in the Works*, published by Simon & Schuster. The book, which contained such prose pieces as "Snore Wife and some Several Dwarts," "Benjamin Distasteful," and "Mr. Boris Morris," received good reviews. Lennon's stories, reminiscent of nursery rhymes, were twisted into bizarre jokes filled with puns.

Still, John felt he could no longer express himself freely. Beatles biographer Bob Cepican claimed that Lennon felt trapped into playing a role that the public expected of him. Just as many of the fans did not hear the words to the songs he played in concert, he felt no one understood him or realized how unhappy he really was.

The Beatles' second movie, *Help!*, was released in July 1965. The film's story, a comedy, focused on the band's escape from a mad scientist and inept religious fanatics, all of whom chase a valuable ring that somehow found its way onto Ringo's finger. No one seemed to ask why John, idolized the world over, rich, famous, and living in a huge mansion, would write such lyrics for the movie's soundtrack as:

> When I was younger, so much younger than today,
> I never needed anybody's help in any way.
> But now those days are gone, I'm not so self-assured,
> Now I find I've changed my mind, I've opened up
>   the doors.
> And now my life has changed in oh so many ways
> My independence seems to vanish in the haze.
> But every now and then I feel so insecure,
> I know that I just need you like I've never done
>   before.

Help me if you can I'm feeling down . . .
Help, I need somebody, Help, not just anybody, help
. . . help!

During this unhappy period of Lennon's life, he and his wife, Cynthia, and George Harrison and his wife, Patti, were introduced to the drug lysergic acid diethylamide (LSD). LSD, also called acid, is an organic compound that induces psychotic symptoms similar to those of schizophrenia. It alters the brain's chemistry and changes the user's perception of reality—in other words, it causes hallucinations.

A friend of George's, who was a dentist in London and with whom the two couples were visiting, put LSD into their coffee without telling them. When the dentist revealed what he had done, the couples insisted upon leaving immediately. More annoyed than concerned about the incident, they decided to drive to a popular nightclub in London. According to Brown, at the club, Lennon and the others experienced bizarre delusions in which they thought they saw the red lights at the club turn into fire and in which the crowd seemed to undulate back and forth.

Unsure of what was happening to them, they decided to return home. It took them hours longer than it should have to drive home because George had trouble driving his car. Cynthia sat in the backseat and stuck her fingers down her throat to induce vomiting, while John talked hysterically to Patti.

When the couples finally returned home, Lennon sat down and began to sketch some drawings. "George's house seemed to be just like a big submarine," he later told Peter Brown, "and I was driving it." As Lennon later suggested in his interview with *Playboy* magazine, he took the potent drug again, but the next time it was by his own choice.

★ "HELP!" ★

On October 26, 1965, the Beatles were presented medals as Members of the Order of the British Empire (M.B.E.). This prestigious award is usually given to important philanthropists (people who promote human welfare; for example, those who give large amounts of money to aid charities) or to people whose achievements have benefited society. The M.B.E. award had never been bestowed upon rock musicians before. Paul, George, and Ringo were thrilled to receive this great honor—John, however, was not. Lennon had always ridiculed the class structure of British society, so he believed that he had become a hypocrite by accepting the award. Ironically, former M.B.E. recipients protested the giving of the award to the Beatles by sending their own medals back to Buckingham Palace. One army officer who returned his medal said he did not want to share his honor with "vulgar nincompoops."

"Army officers get theirs for killing people," Lennon said when he heard about the solider's remark. "We received ours for entertaining. . . . I'd say we deserve ours more." These conflicting feelings— disdain for the establishment but defense of his right to be honored by it—tormented Lennon, who once again felt that he had to compromise himself in order to get ahead in the music world.

Lennon's aunt Mimi proudly displayed the M.B.E. medal on top of the television in the living room of her new seaside home. John had bought the cliffside house in Bournemouth, overlooking a bay of the English Channel, because Mendips—much to Mimi's dismay— had become a regular tourist stop for thousands of Beatles fans.

The way John lived his life made Mimi increasingly unhappy. He smoked marijuana frequently during the recording of the album *Rubber Soul,* which was released in December 1965. Shortly thereafter, according to biographer Albert Goldman, Lennon began using LSD regularly.

For the Beatles the year 1966 was a pivotal one. Their music continued to dominate the charts as each of their new records shot up to number one. On August 5, they

Ringo, John, Paul, and George accept medals as Members of the Order of the British Empire (M.B.E.) on October 26, 1965. Queen Elizabeth II made the presentations at Buckingham Palace to honor the Beatles' achievements. The M.B.E. award had never been given to rock musicians before.

released the album *Revolver*, which is generally considered to be the beginning of a new Beatles sound. Their
musical style, in songs such as "Taxman," "Paperback
Writer," "Eleanor Rigby," and Lennon's "Tomorrow
Never Knows" and "Rain," had moved forward from

A candid photograph offers a glimpse of a Beatles rehearsal. Standing and singing at the piano is Paul. George Martin, the Beatles' producer, stands behind Paul while George Harrison plays the guitar and Lennon plays the harmonica. The Beatles' music continued to dominate the music charts in 1965 and 1966. Lennon, however, became increasingly unhappy and began using LSD regularly.

simple songs and love ballads to more complex chord arrangements. The Beatles also used unusual instruments, such as the Indian sitar (a lute with a long neck and strings), and tried new recording tricks, including John's favorite, dubbing tapes of music played backwards onto the final record, a tactic that had never been used before by a popular rock group.

In the summer of 1966, the group, which was exhausted from rigorous annual world tours, unenthusiastically began another tour to publicize the *Revolver* album. On July 3, 1966, the Beatles landed in Manila, the capital of the Philippines, where a boisterous crowd of more than 50,000 fans greeted them. Routinely declining invitations to government receptions held in the Beatles' honor—since the fiasco at the British Embassy in Washington, D.C.—Brian Epstein ignored an invitation to the group from Imelda Marcos, wife of the country's powerful president, Ferdinand Marcos. The Filipino people did not take the snub kindly, and a riot broke out at the airport when the Beatles tried to leave after their performances. The band was fortunate to get out of the country unharmed. On the way home, they discussed their dissatisfaction with going on tour.

"He's got another world tour already booked for next year," Neil Aspinall, the road manager, told Lennon, referring to Brian Epstein's future plans for the group.

"Nobody can hear a bloody note anyway," John responded in exasperation. Lennon continued, "No more for me. I say we stop touring." The rest of the band agreed with Lennon, and they decided that the August American tour would be their last.

Only four days after their return to England, however, a firestorm of controversy exploded over some comments that Lennon had made earlier. An American teen magazine had reprinted some of his offhanded quotes about religion, and, as a result, John was getting a lot of negative publicity in the U.S. press. The quotes came from a series of articles written by a respected journalist, Maureen Cleave, who had interviewed Lennon for London's *Evening Standard* newspaper. In the interview, she and John talked about topics that were not the usual subjects discussed by rock stars, such as the future of organized religion. "Christianity will go. It will vanish and shrink. I needn't argue about that," Lennon had mused. "We [the Beatles] are more popular than Jesus now. I don't know which will go first—rock and roll or Christianity."

These remarks did not upset English fans, who were accustomed to Lennon's irreverences. In America, however, many people took his remark about the Beatles being more popular than Jesus as an insult. Those newspapers that came to Lennon's defense, including the *New York Times*, interpreted his comments to mean that organized religion was losing members and that there were more people who were Beatles fans than there were people who went to church.

Nevertheless, thousands of the Beatles' records were burned in protest, and their songs were banned from more than 35 radio stations, most of which were located in the Deep South. Occurring on the heels of the fearful

A behind-the-scenes look at the Astoria Theatre in Finsbury Park in London illustrates the boredom and loneliness Lennon began to feel during the Beatles' rise to stardom. A few fans have been admitted to the dressing room by Brian Epstein (standing, center) and excitedly ask for autographs as Lennon and Ringo, looking fatigued, observe the scene.

Manila incident, the protests worried Brian Epstein, who was concerned about Lennon's safety. Epstein hoped that the whole issue could be settled by a public apology—although John would rather have canceled the tour than apologize for his comments. Epstein convinced him to explain what he had meant by his comment about Jesus, so on August 11, 1966, in Chicago, at the start of the Beatles' American tour, Lennon called a press conference to try to clear up the matter.

According to Brown, Lennon appeared pale and nervous as he took the microphone. "If I said television was more popular than Jesus, I might have got away with it," he explained. "I used the word Beatles as

a remote thing, not as what I think. I just said 'they' [the Beatles] had more influence on kids than anything else, including Jesus. I said it in that way, which was the wrong way. I'm not comparing ourselves with Jesus as a person, or God as a thing. I just said what I said, and it was wrong—now there is all this [controversy]."

The reporters looked at each other in confusion. "Yes, but are you prepared to apologize?" a reporter asked immediately.

John thought that was what he had just

On August 9, 1966, people in Waycross, Georgia, burn the Beatles' records after Lennon was quoted as saying that the Beatles were "more popular than Jesus."

done. "I'm not anti-God, anti-Christ, or anti-religion," he replied as his temper flared. "I believe in God, but not as one thing, not as an old man in the sky." He added, "I believe that what people call God is something inside all of us. . . . I wasn't saying the Beatles are better than God or Jesus."

But the press would not let the matter end at that. They asked whether or not he would apologize.

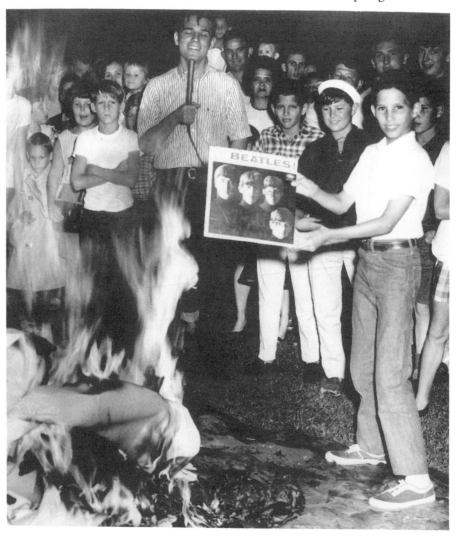

"I wasn't saying whatever they're saying I was saying
. . ." he insisted, then threw his hands up in the air in
frustration. "I'm sorry I said it—really. I never meant it
to be a lousy antireligious thing. . . . I apologize, if that
will make you happy. I still don't quite know what
I've done, but if you want me to apologize, then okay,
I'm sorry!"

At that moment, John decided he had changed his
actions to please other people once too often. Later in the
news conference he publicly criticized U.S. involvement
in Vietnam, but the press was too concerned with his
apology to pay much attention to his controversial remarks about the Vietnam War.

The Beatles played their last series of concerts in
Washington, D.C.; Memphis, Tennessee; Toronto,
Canada; and New York, New York. Their final appearance as a group was at a concert held at Candlestick Park
in San Francisco, California, on August 29, 1966. Although Lennon had been happy to see the tour come to
an end, he was unprepared for idleness when he returned
home. "That's when I really started considering life without the Beatles," he told Andrew Solt in 1980. "What
would I do when it stopped?"

Without any definite plans for his future, he accepted
the role of Private Gripweed in Richard Lester's anti-war
movie entitled *How I Won The War*, filmed in September, in Almería, Spain, and released in 1967. Called
"pretentious tomfoolery" by one critic, the movie
bombed. It also confirmed that Lennon's acting abilities
were not his forte. It was during the filming of this
movie that Lennon took to wearing the oval, wire-framed
"granny" glasses that became his trademark.

In October, he and Cynthia returned from Spain to
their Weybridge mansion. For a long time their marriage
had had its difficulties, and the trip to Spain had not
made their relationship any better. "I knew in my heart,"

Cynthia later wrote in her memoirs, "the loneliness I felt . . . would become a permanent loneliness before very long, and I shivered at the thought."

Bored with his family life and suffering from a lack of musical inspiration, John tried to spur his creativity by cultivating London's art scene. One day, one of his artist friends phoned and invited him to see "Unfinished Paintings and Objects," an avant-garde art exhibition by Yoko Ono at the Indica Gallery. (*Avant-garde* means "vanguard" in French and refers to those artists and writers who are innovators, developing new or experimental concepts in their fields.) His friend's description of the show had intrigued John, especially his report of people rolling around the room in a big plastic bag.

When Lennon arrived at the gallery on the evening of November 9, 1966, he met the artist, Yoko Ono, a Japanese woman less than five feet tall who was dressed in black. She parted her frizzy, waist-long black hair in the middle of her head. "Where's the orgy?" asked John, who thought the show was to be somewhat erotic.

According to Brown, by way of an answer, Yoko handed Lennon a printed card. On it was the word *breathe*. "You mean like this?" he asked, and then panted. She took his arm and led him around the exhibit. At one point he wanted to follow the instructions on a piece of her art that directed the viewer to hammer a nail into wood. Yoko objected to his wish because the exhibit was not officially open yet. "Let him hammer a nail in," the embarassed gallery owner pleaded with her. "Who knows, he might buy it." After a short discussion Yoko agreed to let him do it, but said it would cost John five shillings (then the equivalent of 69 cents).

"Okay," said John, who was both annoyed and amused. "I'll give you an imaginary five shillings, and I'll hammer in an imaginary nail."

Yoko Ono simply smiled.

Lennon drew this portrait of himself and Yoko Ono in 1969. Lennon first met Yoko at her art show at the Indica Gallery in London on November 9, 1966. By this time, Lennon was bored with family life and was suffering from a lack of musical inspiration. Intrigued with Ono, Lennon later agreed to become a patron of her artwork.

Soon after their first meeting, Ono sent Lennon a copy of her book, *Grapefruit*, a compilation of humorous instructional poems that had been published in a limited edition in Tokyo in 1964. Each poem contained advice for the reader, such as "Draw a map to get lost." At first John was annoyed by Ono's writings, but then he became fascinated by them. According to Fred Seaman in *The Last Days of John Lennon* (1991), Ono sent a barrage of letters to Lennon begging for his patronage. He later agreed to provide money for her art shows.

Ono's next art exhibit, in October 1967, was entitled "Half-a-Wind," and comprised everyday objects, such as chairs, beds, and cups, all cut in half. The sponsor of the show was listed as "Yoko plus me" because Lennon did not want his name publicly linked with hers, at least not at this time. He was not quite sure how much he wanted to get involved with her—after all, Yoko Ono was not the answer to whatever it was that he was searching for. Or was she?

6 "Hello, Goodbye"

I N EARLY MARCH 1968, John and Cynthia strolled hand in hand alongside the rushing brown water of the Ganges River near Rishikesh, India, where they were attending a religious retreat. A spark of affection, long missing from their marriage, had just been rekindled by the thoughtfulness of a gift from the Maharishi for young Julian.

The Maharishi Mahesh Yogi, a Hindu spiritual leader, taught Transcendental Meditation, or TM, to the Beatles, their wives or girlfriends, and several other celebrities at the religious retreat he had founded along the banks of the Ganges. The Maharishi's method of TM involved the inward repetition of an incantation, or mantra (sacred sound), to achieve a raised level of awareness. The Maharishi had told the Beatles that by practicing TM regularly, they could open the door to both self-understanding and self-realization—without using drugs. For John, TM offered new hope for finding a way to be at peace with himself.

Lennon first became involved with TM in August 1967, when he had attended a lecture on the subject at a London hotel. The Maharishi, dressed

Yoko Ono clutches Lennon as they leave a London court hearing on October 19, 1968, on charges of possessing marijuana and obstructing police. The couple was released on bail until their trial on November 28.

in a long, flowing white robe, spoke of the possibility of reaching a higher state of consciousness. Believing that TM could offer them happiness, Lennon and the other Beatles went into seclusion for a 10-day course in Bangor, Wales, on August 27.

Two days later, however, tragedy struck, and their course was cut short. The Beatles and their companions had just finished a late lunch and were wandering around the grounds of the campus. During their walk, the group was interrupted by the incessant ringing of the pay phone in the hall of a dormitory. Finally, actress Jane Asher, Paul McCartney's girlfriend, answered it. It was Peter Brown, Brian Epstein's assistant, and he asked to speak to Paul.

"I've got bad news," Brown told him. "Brian is dead. They found him just a little while ago. The press is on to it, so you'd better get back to London."

The authorities declared the official cause of Epstein's death as an accidental overdose of sleeping pills. The public and the press, however, called his death a suicide. "The most tragic part of Brian's death," wrote Brown, "was that here was a man whose passions sparked an entertainment phenomenon—[a man] who had influenced the course of history. But the world would remember his unhappiness, and not the dreams that filled stadiums."

With Cynthia crying at his side, John met reporters coldly—he had learned to become emotionless whenever people close to him had died. Though he and the others had been in Wales for only two days, he claimed, "Our meditation has given us the confidence to withstand such a shock."

Yet within himself Lennon was not so self-assured. "I knew we were in trouble then," he revealed to author Jann Wenner in 1970. "I didn't have any misconceptions about our ability to do anything other than play music—and I was scared."

For the first time in their careers, Lennon and the other Beatles had to take control of their own finances, which they later discovered were in great disarray. Tax and business consultants gave the Beatles advice on how to expand and invest in real estate and practical businesses, such as recording studios and hotels. But the Beatles distrusted and disapproved of most businessmen, whom Lennon called "men in suits," because he saw them as stuffy men who cared only about money. Why not, the Beatles asked themselves, make business fun?

Consequently, the Beatles created Apple Corps, a company that would handle all their financial affairs. The first so-called fun business project they ventured into became Apple Boutique, a clothing store that catered to the mod fashion style—distinguished by short miniskirts, bright colors in bold patterns of paisley or polka dot, wide ties, and wide collars—which was popular when the boutique opened its doors on December 7, 1967. Pete Shotton, John's old friend, managed the store. Shotton had the exterior of the five-story building painted with a huge mural of a young woman's face, complete with stars and a rainbow of colors in the background. The mural upset the conservative shopkeepers in the area, who complained to the authorities, who then had it removed.

Shortly after the company's creation, the Beatles decided that Apple Corps needed to keep up with the changing times of the 1960s and should be more than just an investment company. They wanted to make it a source of financial support for creativity in music, film, publishing, design, and electronics—a kind of foundation—but the company was to make money from various other investments as well. From all over the world, aspiring artists, writers, and musicians deluged Apple with samples of their work and with requests for financial assistance. But the Beatles themselves did not have to

Paul, Ringo, John, and George smile for a photographer in an appearance to mark the release of *Sgt. Pepper's Lonely Hearts Club Band* in 1967. From the beginning of their careers, the Beatles had an unwritten rule that wives and girlfriends were barred from the recording studios while the band worked on its albums. After Lennon's separation from Cynthia in May 1968 he insisted that Yoko be allowed to attend the sessions, which upset the others and created tension in their relationship.

deal with the confusion that resulted: sorting through the chaos was left up to the Beatles' overworked employees in London. After they established the company's goals, the Beatles, accompanied by their wives or girlfriends,

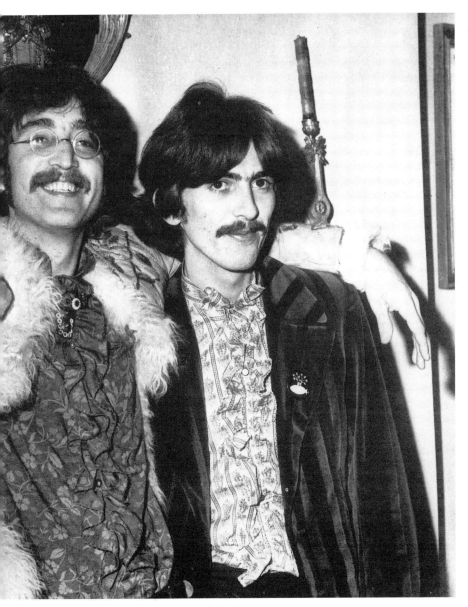

left England in March to seek enlightenment at the Maharishi's Indian retreat.

The religious retreat, called an ashram, located in the remote wilderness of northern India, near the snow-covered Himalayas, was a modern little village unto it-self. It was not a primitive place; it had attractive stone cottages, each of which had four or five bedrooms. The Beatles had been assigned to these heated cottages with modern bathrooms and comfortable beds. At night they could hear the peaceful sound of the Ganges River lapping against its muddy banks. A professional chef prepared vegetarian meals, and servants served the guests at long, carved wooden tables under a vine-covered trellis.

When they had first arrived at the ashram, John and Cynthia told the Maharishi that their son, Julian, would be celebrating his fifth birthday on April 8, 1968, only a few weeks away. The Maharishi surprised the couple the following week with custom-made clothing, worthy of an Indian prince, for Julian. John, apparently thinking about the son he rarely saw, became so moved by the gift that he took Cynthia's hand afterward as they walked along the riverbank.

"Oh, Cyn," he said, feeling a little homesick, "won't it be wonderful to be together with Julian again. Every-thing will be fantastic. I can't wait, can you?"

But when they returned to their sleeping quarters, they went to separate bedrooms—an arrangement John had made before they had arrived at the retreat. Lennon may have looked forward to being back in England again—but not with Cynthia and Julian. Even while he was staying at the Maharishi's remote ashram, he wrote long letters to Yoko Ono.

Cynthia, who was unaware of John's correspondence with Yoko, rejoiced at his good health and improved mood. For the first time since his mother's death, Lennon was free of the drugs and alcohol he had been depending on for consolation. Cynthia thought he looked healthier and happier than ever before. Each night after dinner, John, Paul, and George would sit in the moonlight and play their guitars. (Ringo and his wife, Maureen, left the ashram after 10 days. Maureen could not tolerate the insects that swarmed around the river in the early spring.) Together, they composed an astonishing number of songs—30—that would later appear on their *White Album.*

After six weeks at the retreat, Paul and Jane Asher returned home, having become bored with the long meditation periods. George and John, however, enjoyed the TM course—despite the growing criticism of the Maharishi's motives and sincerity by Magic Alex, John's young Greek artist-inventor friend who was also at the retreat. To undermine the Maharishi's control, Alex smuggled wine into the compound. A short time later a female student at the ashram claimed that the Maharishi had made advances to her in his house.

George, John, and Alex argued about the Maharishi's behavior all through one night until they finally agreed that the Maharishi was using them for publicity purposes and not telling them the truth about his motives. According to Brown, the next morning, John went to the Maharishi to talk with him.

"We're leaving," he told the Maharishi.

"But why?" the Maharishi asked.

"You're the cosmic one," Lennon answered with his typical caustic wit. "You should know."

According to Peter Brown, Lennon grew bitter and disappointed about the whole experience, and TM became yet another endeavor that had not lived up to his high expectations.

On the plane during their trip home from India, John and Cynthia talked about some of their marital problems. While under the influence of scotch and cola, John confessed to having had hundreds of affairs with other women, beginning when he and Cynthia were first dating in Liverpool.

The subsequent tension between the Lennons lasted for several weeks after their return to Weybridge in May 1968. "I felt . . . as though I was sitting on the edge of a volcano," Cynthia later told Peter Brown when she described her mood to him. "John suggested that, as he had to work in the recording studios for a few weeks, I should accompany Alex on a holiday to Greece."

Immediately after Cynthia left for Greece, Lennon began to take LSD again. Pete Shotton later revealed that one evening, while he kept John company after Cynthia had gone, John said to him: "I fancy having a woman around, Pete. Do you mind if I get one in?"

"I don't mind at all," Shotton replied. "I'm not about to stay up another night."

"I think I'll give Yoko a ring, then."

"So you fancy her?" asked Shotton.

"I don't know," Lennon replied. "But there is something about her. I'd just like to get to know her better . . . and now is a good time to do it, with the wife away and all."

Yoko and John spent most of the night talking together and using his tape recorders to create a tape that they later released as an album, entitled *Two Virgins*. Just before dawn, they became lovers.

Cynthia returned home a week later and found Yoko, dressed in Cynthia's bathrobe, casually eating breakfast in the kitchen. Cynthia turned and ran upstairs in tears, realizing that her marriage to John was over.

Yoko Ono was an unlikely rival of Cynthia's. Six years older than John, Yoko, whose name means "Ocean Child" in Japanese, was born in Tokyo, Japan, on February 18, 1934. Her father, a prominent banker, lived in the United States until the Japanese attacked Pearl Harbor on December 7, 1941. After 10 years in Japan, the family moved back to the United States, where Yoko studied philosophy at Sarah Lawrence College, a prestigious school in Bronxville, New York. In 1957, at the age of 23, Yoko eloped with a music composer, Toshi Ichiyanagi, who lived in New York City. Yoko left her husband in 1960 after she had decided to become an avant-garde artist. She returned to Japan in March 1962, where she and Toshi attempted to reconcile. Through him she made contacts in the Tokyo avant-garde art scene.

"I got terrible reviews," she said of her early work. "The conservative elements—men artists and critics—decided to boycott me." When Japanese critics accused her of plagiarizing her ideas from other artists, she grew despondent, and her family hospitalized her to prevent her from committing suicide.

In 1963, Ono divorced Toshi and married Tony Cox at the American Embassy in Tokyo. Cox was an American artist whom she had met in Japan. Lennon biographer Albert Goldman claimed that Yoko Ono indulged in the sexual freedom of the sixties by taking many lovers while she had been married to Toshi Ichiyanagi. But Yoko did not practice birth control because, as she told *Esquire* magazine in 1970, "I was too neurotic to take precautions," and, consequently, she had had several abortions that caused some medical complications. When she became pregnant by Tony Cox, her doctors warned her that another abortion could be dangerous to her health. She decided to have the child, as she explained to Goldman, "because society's myth is that all women are supposed to love children." On August 8, 1963, her daughter, Kyoko, was born.

The Cox family returned to SoHo, a New York City neighborhood where many of the city's artists lived. But the marriage soon deteriorated—and was held together, according to Goldman, only because Tony produced Yoko's art. Goldman also claims that baby Kyoko was physically neglected while Tony and Yoko pursued their individual careers. In September 1966, the Coxes went to London, nearly penniless, to attend an art symposium. One month later, on November 6, Yoko met John Lennon for the first time at the Indica Gallery.

According to Fred Seaman, who became Lennon's personal assistant in 1979, Yoko and John's affair remained secret until May 1968. Meanwhile, in June 1967, the Beatles recorded and released the album *Sgt. Pepper's Lonely Hearts Club Band,* which sold more than 1 million advance copies. The album's colorful cover featured the Beatles dressed as a 19th-century military band, surrounded by life-size cutouts of famous people. The following November they released another record album, *Magical Mystery Tour,* along with a television movie based on the album. Inspired by Paul, the movie turned out to be a poorly filmed account, with no plot, of a bus ride full of strange-looking people and circus characters. It was universally panned by critics. However, John worked hard on the project, and his major contribution was the song "I Am the Walrus."

In June 1968, several weeks after John and Cynthia's separation, the Beatles returned to the Abbey Road studios to record the songs they had written in India while they were at the Maharishi's retreat. By this time, John and Yoko had become inseparable. According to Seaman, Lennon was thrilled by Yoko's aggressive pursuit of him. "I always had this dream of meeting an artist that I would fall in love with," Lennon explained. "Since I was extraordinarily shy, especially around beautiful women, my daydreams necessitated that she [Yoko] be agressive enough to 'save me,' i.e., take me away from all this."

From the beginning of their careers, John, Paul, George, and Ringo had an unwritten rule that wives and girlfriends were banned from the recording studios while the band worked on its albums. But John, unwilling to leave Yoko's side, broke that rule when he allowed Yoko into the studio.

Rather than antagonize Lennon, the other band members tried to ignore the fact that Yoko attended the recording sessions. But Yoko could not sit quietly in the studio and not offer her own strong-willed ideas about the Beatles' music. This interference annoyed Paul and George, who resented her comments about their performances. John, however, expected the others to happily accept direction from his girlfriend. Nevertheless, they considered her completely ignorant of their type of music. Whenever Yoko was at the studio, the other members of the band became sarcastic and cold in their remarks, and behind her back they called her names.

Lennon believed that every wisecrack the others made about Yoko Ono became a personal insult to him. As far as he was concerned, Yoko had given him, in just a few short weeks, more inspiration for his music than the Beatles had given him in eight years. "It seemed," Lennon later told Shotton, "that I had to be either married to them or Yoko. I chose Yoko, and I was right."

To make matters worse, John was unhappy with Paul's "nonprogressive" music and sentimental ballads. George Harrison felt that his own songs were completely ignored by both Lennon and McCartney. Paul became disgusted with John's experimental music, such as the song "Revolution #9," which had no melody and used recordings of noises and repetitive sounds, and John's politically charged song "Revolution." "Revolution," on the other hand, meant more to John than any song he had ever written, because it called for nonviolent, radical political change.

"The statement in 'Revolution' was mine," he proudly told David Sheff of *Playboy*. "The lyrics stand today. They're still my feeling about politics: I want to see the plan. Count me out if it's for violence."

As a result of their personal problems, the Beatles' *White Album* (called "white" because it had been packaged in a plain white cover) recording sessions, in the fall of 1968, were tense and lacked the sense of fun that the group usually had when they recorded together. Ringo Starr became so unhappy, he considered quitting the group. To keep the peace, each of the Beatles used the band to back up their individual songs.

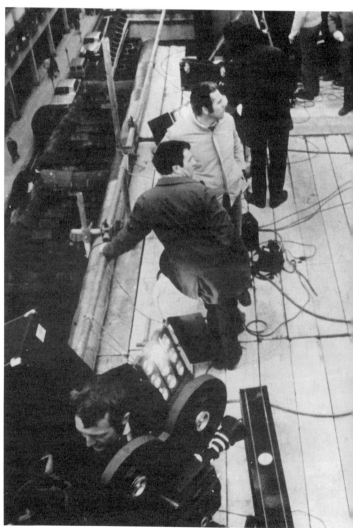

With divorces from their spouses pending and Yoko pregnant with John's child, the two lovers had moved into Ringo Starr's empty apartment on Montagu Square in London during the summer of 1968. There they began to take heroin "as a celebration of ourselves as artists," Yoko later claimed.

"Of course," Peter Brown quoted her as saying, "George [Harrison] says it was me who put John on

Lennon tunes his guitar while film crews take a break from filming the Beatles for *Let It Be* on the roof of the Apple Corps building on January 30, 1969—the last day the Beatles played in public together.

heroin, but that wasn't true. John wouldn't take anything he didn't want to take."

Heroin, an addictive narcotic, soon took over their lives, and John and Yoko lived that summer in the filth and squalor of drug dependency. On October 18, 1968, the police raided their apartment and arrested them for illegal possession of marijuana.

After their release from jail, Yoko was confined to her bed by a doctor, who feared she might miscarry her baby. On November 18, when it was clear to Yoko and John that the baby would not live inside her womb, John recorded the dying baby's heartbeat. Ten days later, Lennon pleaded guilty to drug possession and was fined.

The same day that Lennon had to appear in court, the *Two Virgins* tape, which John and Yoko had made while Cynthia vacationed in Greece, was released as an album with a cover that featured a full-length photo of John and Yoko naked and holding hands. The album revived the scandal of the adulterous lovers' affair. The police in Newark, New Jersey, confiscated 30,000 copies of the record because the local prosecutor declared that the cover was pornographic.

In January 1969, Paul urged the group to come back together to record the album *Let It Be*. He hoped that by filming the band as they recorded the album, the Beatles could recapture the magic that the band had experienced in the early days. But Yoko's presence in the studio, George's obvious resentment over the neglect of his songs, and Paul's constant demands on the group for perfection made the movie of their studio sessions seem more like a documentary of a funeral than a record of the good times.

"Nobody could look at it," Lennon bitterly told Peter Brown afterward, referring to both the sound and film tapes that sat on the shelf for more than a year, unedited. "I really couldn't stand it."

The Beatles played together for the last time in public for the *Let It Be* cameras, on January 30, 1969, out in a cold wind, on the roof of the Apple Corps building at 3 Savile Row in London. John could not resist having the final laugh, though. As the sounds of the song "Get Back" drifted off into the blustery London sky, Lennon leaned forward to the microphone and said: "I'd like to say thank you very much on behalf of the group and myself and I hope we passed the audition."

But the Beatles were simply too big to go their separate ways peacefully. Battle lines had been drawn for one of the most painful and ugly breakups in music history.

7 "Starting Over"

O N MARCH 20, 1969, John Lennon and Yoko Ono were secretly married at the British consulate on the sunny island of Gibraltar, just off the coast of Spain. Both John and Yoko's divorces had been granted; Cynthia had been awarded custody of Julian, and Tony Cox obtained custody of Kyoko.

The couple then flew to Paris, France, where Yoko released the following statement to the press: "We're going to stage many happenings and events together. This marriage was one of them." During their honeymoon in Amsterdam, the Netherlands, the Lennons announced that they planned to promote the cause of peace by spending a week in bed. The first of the couple's bed-ins (as Yoko called the news conferences given to the press while the couple remained in bed) occurred in their honeymoon suite in the Amsterdam Hilton Hotel and lasted seven days. The bed-in, which was billed as a "commercial for peace," had been a publicity effort by Lennon to exploit the media—as he felt he had been exploited by them—by using a news conference to manipulate the press into delivering his message of peace.

On March 20, 1969, John Lennon, with his wife, Yoko Ono, holds up a marriage license after the two were wed on the island of Gibraltar.

In May 1969, the Lennons held their second bed-in, this time in Montreal, Canada. The Lennons had wanted New York as the site of the second bed-in because the United States was deeply involved in the Vietnam War at the time. To his shock, however, John was denied a visa to enter the United States because of his 1968 drug conviction, and he was refused passage on the ocean liner *Queen Elizabeth II.* Still determined to bring their message to America, the Lennons flew to the city of Montreal, which they decided would be close enough to the United States to get the media's attention.

Hordes of reporters, ushered into a flower-filled suite on the 19th floor of Montreal's Queen Elizabeth Hotel, interviewed and photographed the couple in bed. John and Yoko, in matching long hairstyles and dressed in identical stripped pajamas, lay side by side in a white bed. John leaned against fluffy pillows while Yoko affectionately stroked a stuffed teddy bear. Behind them hung a hand-painted sign with the word *Peace.*

The Lennons hold their second bed-in for peace, in Montreal, Canada, on May 26, 1969. The Lennons decided to use the media to make known their pacifist views during the Vietnam War. It was during this bed-in that Lennon wrote the song "Give Peace a Chance."

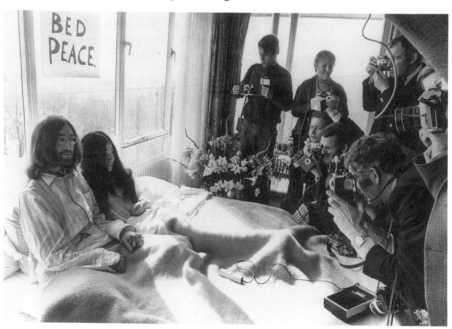

"[They] preach violence all the time in every newspaper, every TV show, and every magazine," claimed John. "The least Yoko and I can do is hog the headlines and make people laugh. We're quite willing to be the world's clowns if it will do any good. People print what I say. And I say, 'Peace.'"

To cap off the Montreal happening, John wrote the song "Give Peace a Chance" and impulsively decided to record it in the hotel room. Such celebrities as the popular psychologist Timothy Leary, the comedian and civil rights activist Dick Gregory, the singers Tommy Smothers and Petula Clark, and a local Hare Krishna religious chapter crowded into the room, which was ablaze with the bright lights set up by film crews.

With the words of the song pasted on the walls, Lennon led the group in singing the song that he hoped would put him smack in the middle of the antiwar movement.

"In my secret heart," he later confessed to Goldman, "I wanted to write something that would take over 'We Shall Overcome.'" (The song "We Shall Overcome" had become an anthem for the civil rights movement.) After recording with Yoko such uncommercial and unsuccessful albums as *Two Virgins* and *Life with the Lions* (1969), Lennon hit the big time with the record single "Give Peace a Chance." Because he put into words the thoughts of millions of young antiwar protesters, the song proved to be a resounding success.

The sense of satisfaction that Lennon received from the popularity of the song kept his spirits up during a trying time—behind the scenes another kind of war was being waged, a war that John helped fuel. The Beatles were breaking up, and the struggle that eventually tore them apart was not over the growing musical differences among John, Paul, and George but over who should control the money.

In February 1969, the Beatles had finally realized that Apple Corps was in financial chaos and that their own finances needed to be guided by an expert. Paul proposed that his girlfriend Linda's father, Lee Eastman, a conservative American lawyer who had some experience in the music business, handle the Beatles' money. His suggestion was met with scorn by the others. Paul could not run the group musically, as he had done after Epstein's death and during John's preoccupation with Yoko Ono, the others told him, and then expect to manage the band through his future father-in-law.

Lennon preferred Allen Klein, an American manager with a reputation for gaining large advances from the record companies for the entertainers he represented. Klein had also acquired a bad reputation after allegations of double-dealing in some business agreements and charges of U.S. tax evasion.

However, Klein's direct and forceful manner impressed John. So did his knowledge of the lyrics to all of the Beatles' songs—Klein even knew which songs John had written. Like Lennon, Klein was orphaned by his mother and raised by an aunt. The two had much in common. Lennon wanted someone to stand up to Paul McCartney and the Eastmans, and Klein seemed to be just the person to do it. George Harrison and Ringo Starr resented Paul's presumptuousness and agreed to hire Klein.

The Beatles never had to discuss financial matters with each other before, because Brian Epstein had always taken care of the business affairs. Bickering between Paul and the others soon cost the Beatles even more money. They missed a chance to acquire NEMS, which had evolved into Brian Epstein's management company, from Brian's brother, Clyde. The purchase of NEMS was important to the Beatles' financial security because NEMS still received 25 percent of the band's earnings.

Unhappy with the turmoil at Apple Corps, Clyde Epstein sold NEMS to Triumph Trust on February 17, 1969. Several months later, Klein bought the business back for the Beatles at a higher price than they would have paid if they had followed the advice of Eastman, who had told them that they should act right away.

In March, during the Amsterdam bed-in, John discovered that the Beatles' song publishing company, Northern Songs, was for sale. In order to keep control of their music, the Beatles needed to buy back a majority of the stock. The attempt to buy the stock eventually drove a wedge between John and Paul after Paul revealed that he had been secretly buying up shares of the stock for several months on the advice of Lee Eastman. John became enraged over Paul's move to gain an unfair advantage over the others.

Allen Klein reviews some business matters with Yoko and John in 1977. In 1969, Lennon and McCartney clashed over who should manage the Beatles' business affairs. Lennon preferred Klein, and McCartney favored Lee Eastman, his future father-in-law. Lennon persuaded Ringo and George to side with him, and Klein became their adviser.

But it was John's temper that lost the deal for the Beatles when he protested the proposed exclusion of Allen Klein from the board of directors of Northern Songs. "I don't see why I should work for a company in which I have no say," Lennon told the other stockholders. He worried that without Klein to represent his interests, he would be taken advantage of. "I'm not going to be messed around by men in suits," he said. Unable to reach a compromise, the controlling portion of stock was sold to Sir Lew Grade in October 1969, and in 1985 it was acquired by Michael Jackson, the American pop star.

Meanwhile, Klein, without Paul's explicit endorsement, had renegotiated the Beatles' record contracts with EMI Records, winning a substantial increase in the group's royalty payments. John, George, and Ringo were so impressed by his dealings that they put him in charge of Apple Corps. Klein promptly fired the unnecessary personnel that the company had acquired during its period of ineffective management.

In July 1969, Lennon reluctantly went back into the studio to record the Beatles' *Abbey Road* album. Despite the animosity among the band members, the money they would earn from the new royalty contract was too good to pass up. Because Yoko was pregnant again and in fragile health, John installed a bed in the studio so they could be near each other. The *Abbey Road* release reassured the public that the Beatles were "alive and well," and it became a commercial success, selling more than 5 million copies.

That summer, Lennon bought Tittenhurst Park, a mansion situated on 74 acres of rolling woodlands and green gardens in Ascot, England. He and Yoko used it as a retreat, where they were determined to kick their heroin habit. "We were very square people in a way," Yoko said in a later interview. "We wouldn't kick in a hospital because we wouldn't let anybody know. We just went cold turkey. Still, it was hard. Cold turkey is always hard."

John composed the autobiographical song "Cold Turkey," about the torment of heroin withdrawal, during a creative period on August 24, 1969. Although its hard, descriptive lyrics, such as "Oh, I'll be a good boy, please make me well / I'll promise you anything, get me out of this hell"—were met with criticism, the song's candor showed courage on John's part. Like a true artist, he had made his music a reflection of his life.

In November, John followed in the footsteps of other M.B.E. recipients who had returned their medals to Queen Elizabeth II. "Your Majesty," he wrote, "I am returning this M.B.E. in protest against Britain's involvement in the Nigeria-Biafra thing, against our support of America in Vietnam, and against 'Cold Turkey' slipping down the charts. With love, John Lennon of Bag."

Although adding the comment about "Cold Turkey" may have cheapened the symbolism of his gesture, Lennon nevertheless continued his peace campaign in December when he had billboards erected in major cities in the United States and England that proclaimed: WAR IS OVER! IF YOU WANT IT.

On the morning of January 26, 1970, Lennon wrote the song "Instant Karma," an expression that refers to the immediate responsibility one takes for one's actions. Not having Paul to help him with the production, John invited Phil Spector, the American record producer, to produce "Instant Karma" as a single. Spector was well

In December 1969, workmen put the finishing touches on a billboard bearing the Lennons' Christmas message for peace in New York's Times Square. Next to the billboard is a U.S. Army recruiting station. John and Yoko had similar signs erected in London, Amsterdam, Athens, Berlin, Los Angeles, Montreal, Paris, Rome, Tokyo, and Toronto.

known for his heavily orchestrated "wall of sound" style, in which the song's background is layered with solid tracks of instruments and backup vocals. He did such a good job with the song that Lennon gave him the musical tapes of *Let It Be*, which had still not been edited, and asked him to produce an album from them.

By now all the Beatles knew their partnership had ended. The four band members had their own projects in the works and rarely spoke to each other. When Spector delivered the *Let It Be* album for the Beatles to listen to, they heard a strange combination of the recording sessions as they had actually happened, with tune-up noises and coughing on one side of the album and songs featuring violins and horns, which were highly polished and heavily dubbed, on the other side. Paul was aghast. His ballad "Long and Winding Road" had been remixed and dubbed with an orchestra and choir. It seemed that Paul, the musical perfectionist, no longer controlled his own music. He decided that this was the last straw.

"I'm doing what you and Yoko are doing," Paul told John on the phone. "I'm putting out an album and I'm leaving the group, too."

"Good," John replied, amused that Paul thought there was a group to leave. "That makes two of us who have accepted it mentally."

In fact, Paul had already recorded an entire album—on which he played all the instruments—at his farm in Scotland. On April 10, 1970, he held a press conference to announce the group's breakup and the release of his own album, entitled *McCartney*. Lennon was furious about McCartney's actions because Lennon had wanted to announce the group's demise the year before but Paul had talked him out of it.

While John brooded at Tittenhurst Park over what he should do next, a book, *Primal Scream, Primal Therapy: The Cure for Neurosis,* arrived in the mail. The book's author, Arthur Janov, was a psychologist in Los Angeles, California. According to Janov, a patient could release personal pain through a series of primordial screams. Janov's theory appealed to John because he and Yoko frequently incorporated screams into their music. Janov claimed that his scream therapy could break down defenses that patients often develop as children to avoid facing painful realities. The sudden deaths of Uncle George, Julia, Stu Sutcliffe, and Brian Epstein were painful memories that John had not yet fully come to terms with.

After John and Yoko attended sessions with Janov in California, the psychologist suggested, as part of the therapy, that John get closer to his son, Julian, with whom John had very little contact. According to Goldman, when Lennon visited the boy at Cynthia's house in England, the housekeeper at Tittenhurst phoned him with the news that Yoko had threatened to take her life because of jealousy over Cynthia. John rushed home to be by Yoko's side.

As unusual as the scream therapy was for John, it did seem to help him. He learned to identify the fears and repressed emotions that he had carried deep within him since his abandonment as a child. However, when Janov tried to film a therapy session, Lennon feared that Janov was just another false prophet, and he decided not to attend any more sessions.

More in touch with his feelings than ever before, Lennon wrote songs in a flurry of creativity. The result was his first solo album, *John Lennon / Plastic Ono Band*, which was released on December 11, 1970. John faced his past in some of the songs on the album, such as "Mother," whose lyrics include: "You had me but I never had you, I wanted you but you didn't want me. . . . Father you left me but I never left you." The most commercially successful song was "God," in which Lennon defined his lifelong disappointments. "I don't believe in Jesus," he sang, "I don't believe in Elvis . . . I don't believe in Beatles . . . I just believe in me."

While Lennon performed solo, Paul McCartney attempted to gain his release from the Apple partnership. He especially wanted to sever all ties with Allen Klein, who now represented the Beatles' interests as a group. The only way to achieve this was to dissolve the agreement Paul had with the other Beatles, but the four disagreed on how to pay the tax liability. Unable to reach a compromise, Paul reluctantly sued the other three musicians on December 31, 1970.

With their money frozen by the court, the Beatles began a series of magazine interviews that turned unpleasant. John and Paul blamed each other for the Beatles' financial problems, and the argument carried over onto their recordings. On his 1971 *Ram* album, Paul alluded to John in the song "Too Many People Preaching Practices" and included a photo of two beetles fighting on the back cover. Later, John responded to Paul on his *Imagine* album with the song "How Do You Sleep," in which he sings to Paul, "The sound you make is Muzak in my ears, you must have learned something in all those years."

On Friday, April 23, 1971, John became involved in a dangerous attempt to kidnap Yoko's daughter, Kyoko. Yoko had only limited access to Kyoko; Tony Cox had been awarded custody at the time of the divorce. The Lennons hired detectives to find Cox and Kyoko, who had moved several times since Tony and Yoko's marriage had ended. When Kyoko was finally located in Palma, Spain, John and Yoko lured her away from a playground and rushed her back to their hotel. Within minutes the Spanish police arrested the Lennons. When the judge asked Kyoko the same difficult question that Fred and Julia had asked John when he was very young—with

Cloaked in black, the Lennons take a brisk walk at Tittenhurst Park, the mansion they bought in Ascot, England. Lennon and his wife used the mansion as a retreat, where they resolved to kick their heroin habit. The lyrics to the song "Cold Turkey" describe the agony of heroin withdrawal.

whom do you wish to live?—little Kyoko replied, "My daddy."

"Yoko loves her daughter," John, disappointed, told reporters afterward, "and I can't let her suffer like this any longer. What effect can all this be having on Kyoko? I remember [when] it was happening to me . . . I was shattered."

Subsequently, Tony and Kyoko moved to the United States and then went into hiding. John and Yoko obtained a court order for Kyoko's custody in the Virgin Islands, which is a U.S. territory, and increased their efforts to find her. In the late summer of 1971, Yoko and John arrived in New York on a six-month temporary visa, but as it turned out, John never went back to England again. While in New York in September, Lennon released the *Imagine* album, whose sensitive title-track lyrics were inspired by one of Yoko's poems.

In addition to his search for Kyoko, Lennon took up a new cause—he became a visible and vocal critic of the U.S. government. Despite his disdain for the constant attention he had once received from the press while he was a Beatle, he now encouraged the media to report his opinions and actions.

At the end of February 1972, Lennon's visa expired, and a protracted battle began with the Immigration and Naturalization Service to allow him to remain in the United States as a resident. The Nixon administration labeled Lennon a threat to national security because of his association with left-wing radicals, such as Abbie Hoffman and Jerry Rubin, and it wanted to deport him. The antiwar movement had become much stronger as more and more people turned against the United States' involvement in Vietnam, and administration officials feared that radicals within the peace movement would try to obstruct the government.

John backed away from his political activism when he became disillusioned with it. "I dabbled in so-called politics," he later confessed, "more out of guilt than anything else. Guilt for being rich, and guilt for thinking that peace and love isn't enough . . . I was doing it against my instincts."

Actually, John's political problems threatened him less than his continued drug addiction. By 1973, he had become pale and bloated in appearance, and his body showed the effects of his abuse. In June, he dismissed Allen Klein as his manager, and then they sued each other. To add to these troubles, Lennon's new album, *Sometime in New York City*, which included such angry songs as "Scumbag," did not sell very well. In April 1973, needing a retreat from a world that seemed hostile to them, John and Yoko bought an apartment suite in the luxurious Dakota building at Central Park West and 72nd Street in New York City.

The Lennons' relationship had become strained and unhappy and their new home did not alleviate their problems. "One night John and I were lying in bed," Yoko recollected for Peter Brown, "and John kept saying how miserable he was, and how he needed to get away. I said that we had been together 24 hours a day for 5 years and that I needed some time apart for myself [as well]. I told him, 'Why not go to Los Angeles?'"

"What would I do there?" John asked.

"Make an album. Call Phil [Spector] and make an album."

"But who would I go with?" he asked. "I can't go by myself."

Yoko already knew the answer to that question: he could go with 23-year-old Japanese-American May Pang, Yoko's secretary and personal assistant. Yoko had convinced Pang that John needed to be guided through a difficult period and that it was okay for them to have an intimate relationship, if one developed, as long as Pang reported everything that happened back to Yoko. When Lennon and Pang left for Los Angeles in September 1973, John thought he had Yoko's approval for the trip, but Yoko later refused to let him return to the Dakota.

In Los Angeles, Lennon wanted to record a "return to roots" album, later entitled *Rock and Roll*, with Phil Spector as the producer. However, John did not realize that Spector was less in control of his life than Lennon was of his. During the taping of the album, Spector acted irrationally and once fired a handgun into the ceiling of the studio. Spector then took all the recordings home with him and refused to come out of his house.

"He's crazy," John said in frustration after suing Spector to recover his tapes. "And he's crazier than me."

Lennon grew discouraged, believing that everything he tried to accomplish seemed destined to be resolved by a lawsuit. Still involved with drugs, Lennon slipped into a pattern of public drunkenness with his rockstar drinking buddies, including Harry Nilsson,

Keith Moon, and Ringo Starr, who had recorded songs with him on *Rock and Roll.* The newspapers had a field day with one of John's antics when, after drinking too much one evening, he was forcibly removed from a nightclub for heckling the Smothers Brothers during their comedy act. This was a low point in Lennon's 18-month separation from Yoko, which he called his Lost Weekend, a phrase used to refer to the blackout period caused by the overconsumption of alcohol.

All the negative publicity he received did not help Lennon in his battle with the Immigration and Naturalization Service. In July 1974, he was again ordered to leave the United States, pending another appeal by his lawyers.

But Yoko's life had not seemed to improve, either. Her art and music careers, which she felt would flourish without John, instead went nowhere. She began to consult an astrologer and tarot card reader before making any decisions.

Meanwhile, she received daily reports from May Pang on John's behavior and physical condition and offered

May Pang and Lennon attend the opening night performance of *Sgt. Pepper's Lonely Hearts Club Band on the Road* at the Beacon Theater in New York on November 18, 1974. The Lennons' relationship became strained, and Yoko suggested that Lennon and Pang, who was Yoko's secretary, take a trip together to Los Angeles, California. During this period, which Lennon called his Lost Weekend, he and Pang had an affair, and he was often seen drunk in public.

specific advice to Pang on how to handle him. However, each time John called Yoko to ask for a reconciliation, she replied, "No, you're not ready."

According to Fred Seaman, the official version of the Lennons' separation was that "Yoko was John's spiritual guide and teacher and his 'banishment' was part of his 'training.' Once John had learned his 'lesson,' Yoko allowed him to move back into the Dakota." Seaman believed that Yoko had pressured Pang into having an affair with Lennon, but Pang soon fell in love with him. After Lennon and Pang moved to Los Angeles, Yoko had become involved with a studio guitarist who helped her record her album *Feeling the Space*. Later, after her disastrous summer concert tour in Japan, Yoko realized she had to get John back.

In August 1974, Lennon and Pang moved back to New York to an apartment on Sutton Place. Realizing that he had been throwing away his health in Los Angeles, he stopped drinking and using drugs for a brief time. During this period he wrote and recorded the *Walls and Bridges* album, upon which rock star Elton John performed. To return the favor, Lennon appeared at Elton John's Thanksgiving Day concert at New York's Madison Square Garden, on November 28, 1974. Yoko Ono watched the performance from a box seat and surprised John in his dressing room after the concert.

"Oh, hello," John said coyly. "Were you here tonight?"

Yoko smiled and let him know that she was still in love with him and might take him back. May Pang watched in dismay as her affair with John ended that night. "Nobody likes to see their situation disappearing," Yoko later explained diplomatically. But Yoko and John did not get back together immediately.

On December 31, 1974, after Pang, Lennon, and his son, Julian, had vacationed in Florida, John said to May, "I guess I should say this to you now. Yoko has allowed me to come home." John gathered his belongings from the apartment and moved back to the Dakota.

In February 1975, the Lennons announced that Yoko was pregnant again. Because of her many miscarriages, she had to stay in bed while John took care of her. This was the beginning of a five-year period in which John became a "house husband" and Yoko handled all their business affairs.

Their son, Sean Ono Taro Lennon, was born on John's birthday, October 9, 1975. "I hadn't seen my first son, Julian, grow up," John lamented to Peter Brown, determined to be a better father to Sean. "I was not there for his childhood at all—and my childhood was something else. I don't know what price one has to pay for inattention to children."

A few years later, John Lennon would pay the highest price possible—with his life—not for inattention to his children but for his fame.

8 "A Part Of Everything"

BY THE BEGINNING OF DECEMBER 1980, the bright-colored leaves of autumn had fallen from the trees in New York City's Central Park. Across the street from the park, at Central Park West and 72nd Street, Mark David Chapman stared up at the gritty bricks of the Dakota apartment building.

Chapman, pudgy and overweight, wore glasses, and his baby face made him look younger than his 25 years. He had grown up in a suburb of Atlanta, Georgia, where friends remember him as an average teenager who had interests in flying saucers and rock and roll music. Imitating the Beatles, he grew his hair long and learned to play the guitar. In high school, someone introduced him to hallucinogenic drugs, and he took them often.

Suddenly, in 1969, Chapman became deeply religious. He stopped taking drugs, sold his Beatles' records, read the Bible frequently, and wore a large wooden cross on a chain around his neck. According to Andrew Solt, Chapman once criticized Lennon's song "Imagine" at a church prayer

John, Yoko, and their son Sean pose for a photograph in their Palm Beach, Florida, retreat. For more than five years, from 1975 to 1980, Lennon did not release an album of new material, preferring instead to be a "house husband."

meeting, calling it blasphemous because of its lyrics: "Imagine there's no heaven, it's easy if you try / No hell below us, above us only sky."

After his graduation from high school, Chapman became a very popular children's camp counselor at a YMCA in Arkansas. In June 1975, hoping to someday become a Christian missionary, Chapman went to work in a YMCA in Beirut, Lebanon. Almost as soon as he arrived there, however, a civil war broke out, and all YMCA personnel were sent back to the United States. Before he departed, Chapman recorded the sounds of the gunfire outside his hotel room.

When he returned home, Chapman attended college, but a nervous breakdown caused him to drop out after less than a semester. After he recovered from his illness, he went to work at a Vietnamese refugee placement center in Arkansas, but the center closed in December 1975. Chapman then trained for a new job as a security guard, at which time he learned to shoot a pistol.

According to Goldman, Chapman's thinking became more and more confused, and a few weeks after he moved to Hawaii in 1977, he attached a hose to the exhaust of his car and tried to kill himself. He was hospitalized for "severe neurotic depressive reaction" and continued to receive outpatient care for his mental condition after his release from the hospital.

In the summer of 1978, Chapman used some money his father had given him to take a trip around the world. The following year, he married Gloria Abe, the Japanese-American travel agent who had made the arrangements for his trip.

For a short time he lived a normal life, but his mental condition deteriorated and by December 1979, he had quit his job in a hospital's print shop and took work as a security guard, where co-workers later claimed he stayed to himself and became intensely interested in guns.

One of Chapman's acquaintances later described Chapman to Goldman as "a creep, a negative, a cold [and] ugly person." Slowly slipping from reality, Chapman telephoned threats of "Bang! Bang! You're dead," to a nearby church, which he believed was brainwashing people.

Chapman left his security guard job, without notice, on October 23, 1980, signing the company ledger with the name "John Lennon" instead of his own. Four days later, he bought a .38-caliber special, a snub-nosed five-shot revolver, from a Honolulu gun store, which advertised, "Buy a gun and get a bang out of life." When an employment agency called Chapman to ask if he would like a new position, Chapman replied, "No, I already have a job to do."

On October 30, 1980, he arrived in New York City and began to stalk his target, John Lennon, whom Chapman believed was "a symbol of the phonies of this world." Chapman was under the delusion that he was like Holden Caulfield, a fictional character from J. D. Salinger's novel *Catcher in the Rye* (1951). In the story, Caulfield is a bright but naive young man who is expelled from preparatory school and decides to go to New York City. Caulfield is disgusted by what he sees as an adult world filled with phoniness, pretense, and perversion. He rebels and becomes the "catcher" of small children, a defender against corruption.

According to Goldman, Chapman first chose Lennon as a target in October 1980 after reading an article in *Esquire* magazine about Lennon's alleged interest in making money rather than music. The article apparently gave Chapman the idea that he now had the proof that Lennon should die.

But Chapman did not know that after John and Yoko had reunited in January 1975, it was Yoko who took care of all their financial affairs. "It was good for me to do the business and regain my pride about what I could do," she later told David Sheff of *Playboy*. "And it was good to know what he needed. The role reversal; that was so good for him." It was she who had invested in New York State dairy farms and a large mansion, called El Solano, in Palm Springs, Florida, among other real estate. According to Fred Seaman, Yoko controlled all of John's money and made all business decisions after consulting her psychic advisers.

Besides Chapman's misconception about Lennon's insincerity in his business dealings, Chapman also saw Lennon as having a negative influence on children. According to psychiatrists who questioned Chapman later, Chapman came to believe that it was his duty to save children from a corrupt world by killing John Lennon and that by accomplishing this task, Chapman would become a hero.

Lennon, however, had very little influence on the public at all. After Lennon was finally granted a permanent U.S. residence visa in 1976, he withdrew from the public eye—and from the music scene as well. He became a virtual prisoner of the Dakota, hardly venturing out at all. And when he did, he worried about being recognized by some overzealous fan, who would try to touch him or who would hound him for an autograph. In his *Last Days of John Lennon*, Seaman writes, "Yoko had the key to John Lennon, and she used it to make John her sole possession by taking him out of public circulation. The old lion [Lennon] had pulled in his claws eagerly and agreed to give up rock and roll and its deleterious lifestyle. Because of his self-destructive behavior when he was on his own, John believed that the only sane alternative was to isolate himself."

When Lennon returned from the Lost Weekend, he no longer made music, he later claimed, because he preferred to stay at home with Sean. "The joy is still there," John is reported to have said in an interview, "because I've attended to every meal, and how he sleeps, and the fact he swims like a fish because I took him to the ocean. I'm so proud of all those things. But he is my biggest pride."

For more than five years, from 1975 to 1980, Lennon did not release an album of new or original material, and he responded angrily to the criticism that Yoko was the person responsible for his lack of musical creativity during that time. "Anybody who claims to have some interest in me as an individual artist," he said, "or even as a part of the Beatles, has absolutely misunderstood everything I ever said if they can't see why I'm with Yoko."

It was not until June 1980, when Lennon sailed with a small crew to the island of Bermuda, that John found the inspiration to write music and sing again. The Bermuda sunshine and the driving musical rhythms of reggae—the popular style of music from Jamaica that combines the traditional music of the islands with elements from rock and roll and soul music and accents the offbeat—renewed his creative energy. He immediately phoned Yoko, who had stayed behind at the Dakota, anxious to record an album again.

John and Yoko decided to share the new album, each writing their own songs—Yoko in New York and John in Bermuda. Among the songs John wrote were "Woman," "Starting Over," and "Watching the Wheels." Yoko's included "Hard Times Are Over," "I'm Your Angel," and "Kiss, Kiss, Kiss." After Lennon had returned to New York and was back in the studio, he, Yoko, and their record producer mixed the songs to create *Double Fantasy*, which was released on the Geffen Records label on November 17, 1980. (The name for the album had come from a patch of orchids Lennon had happened upon while he, Sean, and some companions had been walking in the Bermuda Botanical Gardens.)

Yoko and John kiss. The Lennons chose this photograph for the cover of their joint album, entitled *Double Fantasy*, which was released in November 1980. John wrote the songs "Woman," "Starting Over," and "Watching the Wheels" after being inspired during a vacation in Bermuda with Sean.

Two months before the album's release, the Lennons began to aggressively promote *Double Fantasy*, and to everyone's surprise, Lennon came out of seclusion to give interviews to an astonished press. With newfound enthusiasm for work, Lennon then returned to the studio to produce a single for Yoko entitled, "Walking on Thin Ice."

Meanwhile, on November 11, 1980, Mark David Chapman won an important battle that had been raging in his mind, a battle between the forces of good and evil. From New York he called his wife in Hawaii and said that he had made a mistake. "I have won a great victory," he told her. "I'm coming home." According to Goldman, after Chapman returned to Hawaii he told his wife that the whole episode in New York had been a bad dream. He spent the next three weeks watching television.

But by Sunday, December 7, Chapman had returned to New York City and checked into a room at the Sheraton Centre Hotel. According to Goldman, Chapman bought a copy of *Catcher in the Rye* on Monday morning and wrote, "This is my statement," inside the front cover of the book.

Chapman arrived at the Dakota at 10:30 A.M. on December 8, clutching the Salinger book and the album *Double Fantasy* under his arm. As the winter's darkness spread over the city just after 5 P.M., Lennon finally came out of the Dakota to go back to the recording studio. Paul Goresh, an amateur photographer and ardent Lennon fan, took a photograph of Lennon as John autographed Chapman's copy of *Double Fantasy*. On the album cover Lennon wrote "John Lennon 1980" as Chapman looked on sheepishly. Goresh later told the police that Chapman had said to him after Lennon left, "They'll never believe this in Hawaii."

At 10:50 P.M., the Lennons' limousine pulled up to the front entrance of the Dakota. Alone now, Mark David Chapman waited in the shadows of the Dakota while the building's doorman, José Perdomo, held the car door open for Yoko. When Lennon emerged and brushed past him, Chapman took two steps forward and raised his gun with both hands to fire. Without saying a word, he pulled the trigger five times. The first two bullets caught Lennon in the back, two more entered his shoulder, and the fifth one missed its target.

Yoko screamed as John staggered up the stairs of the vestibule, blood pouring from his open wounds. Chapman dropped the gun on the sidewalk and stood there, holding only the paperback book and silently waiting for the police to arrive.

"Do you know what you just did?" cried Perdomo to Chapman.

"I just shot John Lennon," Chapman replied quietly.

Lennon was rushed in a police car to Roosevelt Hospital, but no amount of heroic effort on the part of the doctors could save his life.

According to Goldman, the psychiatrists who examined Chapman later reported that he suffered from a "grandiose sense of self-importance, fantasies of success, power, and ideal love, indifference to the feelings of others, [and] a need for constant attention and admiration." They concluded that Chapman's desire to become famous was his primary motive for the murder.

In the early hours of December 9, 1980, Yoko Ono leaves New York's Roosevelt Hospital after being told of her husband's death.

On June 22, 1981, Mark David Chapman pleaded guilty to murdering John Lennon and is serving a sentence of 20 years to life at Attica State Prison, near Buffalo, New York.

Almost immediately after hearing the news of Lennon's tragic death, the world began to mourn one of its greatest musical geniuses. Thousands of fans, held back by police barricades, kept vigil in Central Park, across the street from the Dakota. Crying, they sang "Give Peace a Chance," which had become an anthem for all those who believed in nonviolence.

A courtroom drawing depicts Mark David Chapman (left) holding a copy of J. D. Salinger's *Catcher in the Rye.* Chapman pleaded guilty to murdering Lennon and is serving a sentence of 20 years to life at Attica State Prison.

Six days after Lennon's death, on Sunday, December 14, 1980, people around the world held a 10-minute tribute to John Lennon according to Yoko's wishes. More than 100,000 fans gathered in Central Park to observe this period of prayer and meditation. On October 9, 1985, Yoko Ono donated $1 million to New York City to have the gathering place in Central Park made into a small garden and dedicated as Strawberry Fields, in memory of John Lennon.

During his life, John Lennon had been proud to be recognized for his contributions to the peace movement, but the public remembers him best for the music he gave them. He is considered by many to be the greatest rock musician in the world. From 1964 to 1970, the Beatles had 60 songs on the U.S. charts, and more than half of them were in the top 10—selling 85 million LPs and 120 million singles. Three generations have listened to Lennon's songs—songs that speak with a depth of compassion, caring, and understanding for his fellow human beings. Lennon's musical style and talent have influenced countless other musical groups, including the Rolling

Stones and Guns N' Roses, and have been sung by such diverse performers as Frank Sinatra and Willie Nelson.

Lennon's tragic death signaled the end of an era. But the legacy of his music and his dedication to peace live on, especially in the hearts and minds of his two children. Lennon's son Julian has become a successful rock star in his own right. He paid tribute to his father on his album *Valotte* with his poignant song "Too Late for Goodbyes,"

More than 100,000 people gathered in Central Park on December 14, 1980, during a silent vigil for the slain Lennon. Five years later, after receiving a donation from Yoko, New York City made a small garden at the gathering place and dedicated it to John's memory as Strawberry Fields.

which remained on the top 40 list for 29 weeks in 1984. Lennon's son Sean, who was five years old when his father was killed, the same age John was when his own father, Fred, abandoned him, has only his childhood memories of Lennon. When the five-year-old Sean tried to understand what his father's death meant, he explained, "Now daddy is part of God. I guess when you die, you become much more bigger because you're a part of everything."

Discography ★ ★ ★ ★ ★ ★ ★ ★ ★ ★ ★ ★ ★ ★ ★ ★ ★

(Based on American albums and release dates)

Original Beatles Albums:

Meet The Beatles! (1/20/64)

The Beatles Second Album (4/10/64)

A Hard Day's Night (6/26/64)

Something New (7/20/64)

Beatles '65 (12/15/64)

The Early Beatles (3/22/65)

Beatles VI (6/14/65)

Help! (8/13/65)

Rubber Soul (12/6/65)

"Yesterday" . . . and Today (6/20/66)

Revolver (8/8/66)

Sgt. Pepper's Lonely Hearts Club Band (6/2/67)

Magical Mystery Tour (11/27/67)

The Beatles ("The White Album") (11/25/68)

Yellow Submarine (1/13/69)

Abbey Road (10/1/69)

Let It Be (5/18/70)

John Lennon Solo Albums:

Unfinished Music No. 1—Two Virgins (11/11/68)

Unfinished Music No. 2—Life with the Lions (5/26/69)

The Wedding Album (10/20/69)

John Lennon/Plastic Ono Band (12/11/70)

Imagine (9/9/71)

Sometime in New York City (6/12/72)

Mind Games (10/29/73)

Walls and Bridges (9/26/74)

Rock and Roll (2/17/75)

Shaved Fish (10/24/75)

Double Fantasy (11/17/80)

Milk and Honey (1/19/84)

John Lennon—Menlove Avenue (9/86)

John Lennon—Live in New York City (1986)

Further Reading ★ ★ ★ ★ ★ ★ ★ ★ ★ ★ ★ ★ ★ ★ ★

Baird, Julia, and Geoffrey Giuliano. *John Lennon, My Brother.* New York: Holt, Rinehart and Winston, 1988.

Best, Pete, and Patrick Doncaster. *Beatle! The Pete Best Story.* New York: Dell, 1985.

Brown, Peter, and Steven Gaines. *The Love You Make.* New York: McGraw-Hill, 1983.

Davies, Hunter. *The Beatles: The Authorized Biography.* New York: McGraw-Hill, 1978.

Epstein, Brian. *A Cellarful of Noise.* In Rock & Roll Remembrances series, No. 4. London: Pierian Press, 1984.

Garbarini, Vic, Brian Cullman, and Barbara Graustark. *Strawberry Fields Forever: John Lennon Remembered.* New York: Bantam Books, 1980.

Goldman, Albert. *The Lives of John Lennon.* New York: Bantam Books, 1989.

Green, John. *Dakota Days.* New York: St. Martin's Press, 1983.

Martin, George. *All You Need Is Ears.* New York: St. Martin's Press, 1979.

Pang, May, and Henry Edwards. *Loving John.* New York: Warner, 1983.

Seaman, Frederic. *The Last Days of John Lennon.* New York: Dell, 1991.

Sheff, David, and G. Barry Golson. *The Playboy Interviews.* New York: Playboy Press, 1981.

Shotton, Pete, and Nicholas Schaffner. *John Lennon in My Life.* New York: Stein & Day, 1983.

Solt, Andrew, and Sam Egan. *Imagine.* New York: Macmillan, 1988.

Wenner, Jan. *Lennon Remembers.* New York: Fawcett Books, 1971.

Wiener, Jon. *Come Together.* New York: Random House, 1984.

Chronology ★ ★ ★ ★ ★ ★ ★ ★ ★ ★ ★ ★ ★ ★ ★ ★

1940	Born John Winston Lennon on October 9 in Oxford Street Maternity Hospital, Liverpool, England
1945	Lennon is taken in by his mother's sister Mimi and her husband, George Smith
1957	Meets Paul McCartney at a performance of Lennon's group, the Quarry Men; Paul joins the group a few weeks later
1958	Lennon's mother is killed by a speeding car; George Harrison joins the Quarry Men
1960	Debut of the Beatles—John, Paul, and George on guitars, Pete Best on drums, and Stu Sutcliffe on bass—in Hamburg, West Germany
1961	Debut of the Beatles in England; Brian Epstein becomes their manager
1962	Stu Sutcliffe dies; Pete Best is replaced by Ringo Starr; John marries Cynthia Powell on August 23
1963	The Beatles' single, "Please Please Me," rises to number one in England; John's son, John Charles Julian Lennon, is born on April 8
1964	The Beatles' American television debut on "The Ed Sullivan Show"; *In His Own Write*, Lennon's first book, is published; filming begins on *A Hard Day's Night*
1965	*A Spaniard in the Works* is published; *Help!* premieres; the Beatles are awarded the M.B.E., Britain's highest civilian honor
1966	Lennon's remarks on Christianity cause a storm of protest in the United States; the Beatles' final concert is held in San Francisco, on August 29; Lennon meets Yoko Ono
1967	*Sgt. Pepper's Lonely Hearts Club Band* album is released and is hailed by critics as a revolution in music; the band meets the Maharishi Yogi and attends a Transcendental

Meditation (TM) course; Brian Epstein dies of a drug overdose

1968 The Beatles travel to India to study TM with the Maharishi; John begins an affair with Yoko Ono; Cynthia is granted a divorce and gains custody of Julian; Yoko becomes pregnant and miscarries

1969 The Beatles' last performance together, during the filming of *Let It Be*; John marries Yoko on March 20; the Plastic Ono Band, comprised of John, Yoko, and friends, records "Give Peace a Chance," during the Lennons' "bed-in" for peace; the Beatles record the *Abbey Road* album; Lennon returns his M.B.E. medal to protest the Vietnam War

1970 Paul McCartney announces the demise of the Beatles and later sues to end the Beatles' partnership

1971 Lennon records the song "Imagine"; the Lennons move to New York after being arrested in Spain for the attempted kidnapping of Yoko's daughter; the Nixon administration attempts to have Lennon deported because of his politics

1973 The Lennons buy an apartment in the Dakota in New York City; Lennon leaves for Los Angeles with May Pang, beginning an 18-month separation from Yoko

1974 The Beatles are officially dissolved; Lennon returns to Yoko

1975 Sean Ono Lennon is born in New York City on Lennon's 35th birthday

1976 Lennon wins the right to stay in the United States permanently; begins a five-year period in which he writes no music and claims he has become a "house husband"; Yoko runs their business affairs

1980 Lennon begins to write songs again and produces a successful new album with Yoko, *Double Fantasy;* on December 8, Lennon is shot and killed by Mark David Chapman outside the Dakota

Index ★

PICTURE CREDITS

Leeza Gibbons is a reporter for and cohost of the nationally syndicated television program *Entertainment Tonight* and NBC's daily talk show *John & Leeza from Hollywood.* A graduate of the University of South Carolina's School of Journalism, Gibbons joined the on-air staff of *Entertainment Tonight* in 1984 after cohosting WCBS-TV's "Two on the Town" in New York City. Prior to that, she cohosted "PM Magazine" on WFAA-TV in Dallas, Texas, and on KFDM-TV in Beaumont, Texas. Gibbons also hosts the annual "Miss Universe," "Miss U.S.A.," and "Miss Teen U.S.A." pageants, as well as the annual Hollywood Christmas Parade. She is active in a number of charities and has served as the national chairperson for the Spinal Muscular Atrophy Division of the Muscular Dystrophy Association; each September, Gibbons cohosts the National MDA Telethon with Jerry Lewis.

Bruce W. Conord is a graduate of Rutgers University and a freelance writer. His articles have appeared in several national magazines and newspapers, including the *Trenton Times* and the *Cleveland Plain Dealer.* He is the author of *Cesar Chavez* and *Bill Cosby* in the Chelsea House JUNIOR WORLD BIOGRAPHIES series. He has been a fan of John Lennon's since he first heard "I Want To Hold Your Hand" played on his old static-filled AM radio in 1964, and his son Christian has an extensive collection of Beatles memorabilia. Mr. Conord currently resides with his wife in Hightstown, New Jersey.